The Possibility of Tenderness

The Possibility of Tenderness

A Jamaican Memoir of Plants and Dreams

JASON ALLEN-PAISANT

HUTCHINSON
HEINEMANN

HUTCHINSON HEINEMANN

UK | USA | Canada | Ireland | Australia
India | New Zealand | South Africa

Hutchinson Heinemann is part of the Penguin Random House group of companies
whose addresses can be found at global.penguinrandomhouse.com

Penguin Random House UK,
One Embassy Gardens, 8 Viaduct Gardens, London SW11 7BW

penguin.co.uk

Penguin
Random House
UK

First published 2025
001

Typeset in 12/14.75pt Dante MT Std by Jouve (UK), Milton Keynes
Printed and bound in Great Britain by Clays Ltd, Elcograf S.p.A.

The authorised representative in the EEA is Penguin Random House Ireland,
Morrison Chambers, 32 Nassau Street, Dublin D02 YH68

A CIP catalogue record for this book is available from the British Library

ISBN: 978-1-529-15362-0

To Mama, and to them other ones I'm trying to know.

For Joy and for Imani.

*meanwhile, on every level the rooted ones grew. some called them
tree people for the way they stayed planted, grew horizontally,
shed colorful revelations every season onto the same ground.*

—Alexis Pauline Gumbs

*Beauty is not a luxury, rather it is a way of creating
possibility . . . a transfiguration of the given. It is a will to
adorn, a proclivity for the baroque, and the love of too much.*

—Saidiya Hartman

Contents

1. Mama's Grung   1
2. A People's History of the Land   19
3. Quiet Bonds   47
4. The Teachings of Plants   61
5. Archival Detective   95
6. The Poetry of Monuments   114
7. Gathering the Dispersed   134
8. Miss Ivey's Garden   158
9. Walking in England   176
10. Mama's Salindine   194
11. On the Veranda of the Great House   215

   Epilogue   228
   A Note on Sources   236
   Acknowledgements   239

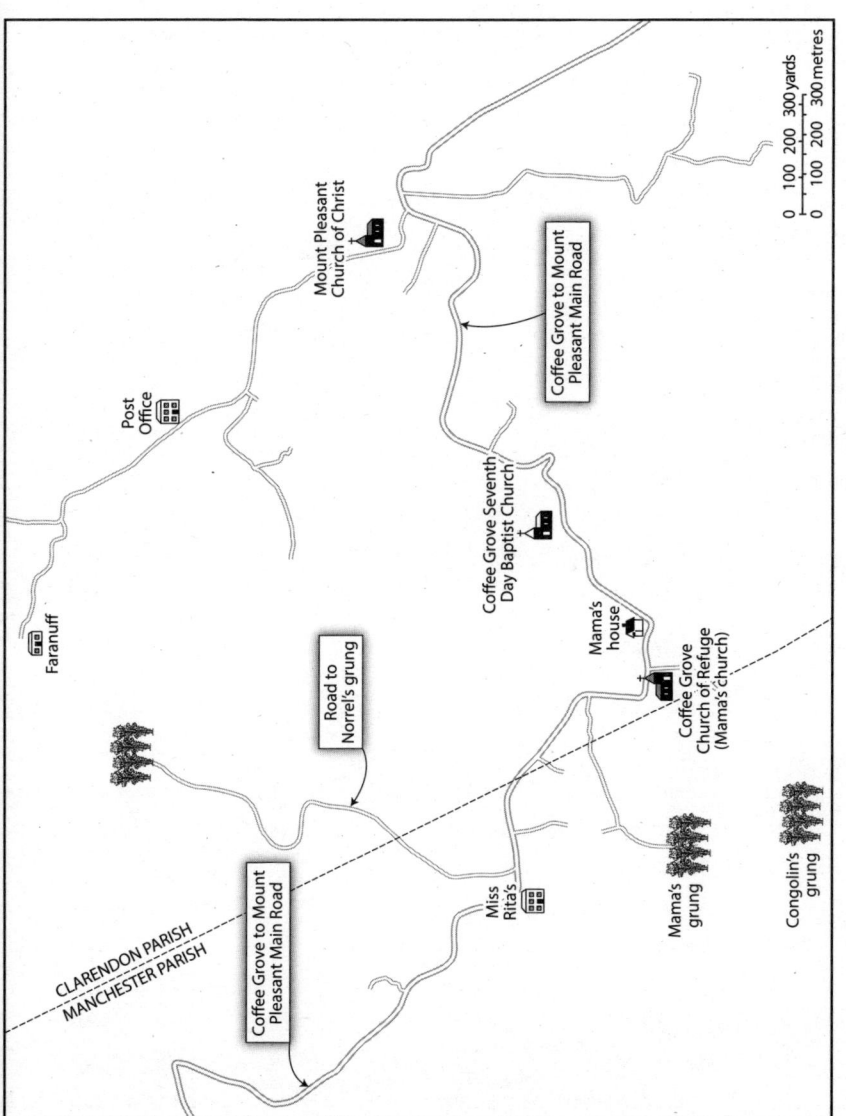

The places of this book as shown on this map.

Mama's Grung

When I was a child growing up in Coffee Grove, Jamaica, I knew trees by climbing them. If they were unclimbable, I looked at them longingly. I threw stones to down their fruit or cut bamboo poles to hook them. These were trees that fed us. We gave short shrift to the ones that bore no food. I counted them off on our way to grung – mango, coconut, guinep, breadfruit, star apple, guava. In Jamaica, grung is our name for the small cultivation plots of peasant farmers, but also for anywhere food crops grow. Grung is synonymous with 'earth', and 'earth' holds profound significance in the belief systems passed down to us by our African ancestors; food is part of an overall cycle of connection with the soil. Though many aspects of this cycle, including the rituals that celebrate the earth, have been overshadowed by the religion brought by the European colonisers, this intuitive sense of connection with the soil endures. It persists every time we say the word *grung*. For me, grung was where Mama planted yams. Mama was my maternal grandmother, but she raised me, so that up till the age of five I thought she was my actual mother.

The guango was a dark tree: tall, fat and unclimbable. It evoked a feeling of smallness, though not a humiliating one. There was a sadness that it gave me, a feeling, at once, of being extracted from the flow of life and yet of being most deeply embedded in it. The poet Ross Gay has characterised joy as a feeling 'infused with the act of dying', and I find in his words a language for describing the sensations the guango tree produced in me: 'act of dying' is Gay's way of describing 'the feeling of disappearing into and profoundly joining something'. What I felt upon contact with the guango tree was, indeed, a feeling of dissolution and absorption into the tree, into the green and ochre world around me, as I walked through the fields with Mama.

Coffee Grove is located in the north of the parish called Manchester, close to the border with Clarendon. It's a hilly area, sitting high up in the May Day Mountains. At this altitude, 591 metres above sea level, it enjoys cool temperatures for much of the year, which makes it an ideal location for growing the plant that gives it its name. Excepting the odd family that keeps a few coffee trees for their personal consumption, hardly any coffee is grown here any more. A rural district, as we call villages in Jamaica, its population of a few hundred people live in houses scattered along a stretch of mountain, or down the small dirt tracks hidden here and there along the road that snakes up into the Cockpit Country, with the village of Blue Mountain to the south and the district of Mount Pleasant above it. A small, sparsely strewn settlement, where everybody knows each other but your nearest neighbour might be well out of earshot. A couple of churches and half a dozen wooden shacks selling household essentials like bleach, soap powder and flour. For the rustic joviality of rum bars, you can go to either Mount Pleasant or Blue Mountain: Coffee Grove is a devoutly Christian place, where the elders frown upon drinking and 'carousing'.

For the entirety of my early childhood, the district had no electricity. It had no piped water either, and still doesn't today. Nights there had the sort of deep silence that summoned up tales of roving spirits called rolling calves – bulls with flaming eyes – and other mythical creatures that terrified us. They were the first stories that fired my imagination and they inhabit it even today.

Yet the silence was far from total. In these streets devoid of electric lamps and nocturnal gatherings, a sort of music would emerge, the sounds of crickets, pattoos and peenie wallies. Only later, when I went to live with my birth mother in the nearby town of Porus, would I experience jukeboxes blaring rocksteady and 'oldies' from Bagga's, the rum bar near our home.

Coffee Grove is a quiet, slow, rural district, and if you live here, chances are your life is organised around the grung. The Coffee Grove Church of Refuge, the born-again, tongues-speaking church, will probably represent a sort of compass in your world. Today, many of the young have emancipated themselves from it, but for generations their parents had sworn allegiance to, and were often subjugated by, its strict moralism and demon-rebuking devotion. With such religiosity, there's a part of youth that dies as soon as it appears.

Coffee Grove is both a tiny place and a huge planet. It's full of traces. It's a universe from which I make sense of the world I move in. It is a *version* of Jamaica, but a significant one that many people have never heard about via the media or in books. It's not the tourist paradise, not the Jamaica sold as *sun, sand and sea*. Nor is it the police raids and shoot-outs, the ghettos, the neglected inner-city communities of Kingston or Montego Bay. It's a Jamaica that has struggled to exist and to continue existing, fighting amidst the challenges posed by globalisation.

★

The district is full of hills, and to reach Mama's grung, we climbed one. This hill was nameless. It was steep and full of rocks, difficult, like most of the other paths we had to travel. On weekday mornings, we'd climb the hill that led to Mount Pleasant, where Mama was the mistress of the postal agency which also served Coffee Grove. Crawling into the mind of that child of three, four or five, I see myself now, walking up and over two significant hills, the one that leads to the grung, and the one that takes us up to Mount Pleasant. Under scorching heat. The rains come often enough; nobody complains. It is also a rainy land. Abundant, green. The crops grow, the farmers work. *Percy werk.* Mama told me that that was my first sentence. *Percy is working*, Percy being a friend of hers whose house lies along the road. And I roll the *tonkit*, my word for the shrivelled, dried coconuts that fall along the roadside – child's play to make the journey more bearable for my tiny legs.

Whatever road we travel – the hill leading to Mama's grung, or the one leading to the postal agency in Mount Pleasant, or the many other paths that branch off that narrow, meandering main road linking Coffee Grove to the rest of the world – the red ground runs beside us: the scarlet, bauxite-rich earth filled with potato slips, tomato beds, carrots, cabbages and all sorts of growing foods with which this thriving agricultural district fed itself . . . and yams! Acres and acres of yams growing under scarlet hillocks. On hillsides, beside roads, in gullies – yams as far as the eye can see. Over ten varieties – the pride of every farmer. Long, red grung under the sun, backs bent, heat parching skin.

Go now into the body of the five-year-old child, to look through his eyes. As soon as you come off the brow of the hill that leads to Mama's grung and enter the vast clearing, there is the guango tree before you on your left. To get to the grung at the end of this track, we pass just under the guango, then turn off to the right, through someone else's pasture. We go up through this pasture to the common mango tree. The grung is before us – a half-acre of land.

Mama had knowledge of the grung. She worked the land by herself. When she had help, it was minimal. She would pay to have the yam sticks cut and erected, and if the sticks weren't to her liking, the men would have to bring new ones; she'd tell them off. A few times a year – in May, August and December – men would come to mulch the hillocks and to help when there was a huge amount of yam planting to do: these months were the best months for planting. Timing is everything for yams: different yams are planted at different stages of the moon, and they need different amounts of time – sometimes vastly different – to be optimally mature. There's an inherited science when it comes to yam cultivation; you don't just get up one day and say you're doing it.

If I step over into my childhood memory, Mama is often clutching an almanac, quietly murmuring to herself. She's sitting on her bed or on her wooden bench on the veranda, muttering words whose connections I don't fully understand: *full moon, first quarter, second quarter, third quarter; dark night . . . new moon; Sinvinsen, mozella . . . to dig; afu fi go in dark night.* These mutterings were like spells, and yet I knew – at three, four years old – that they were plans – instructions to self – for planting. Holding the almanac while speaking to herself seemed as much a 'Mama thing' as her mulching the yam hills or training their vines, as her sourcing from friends the goat's milk that she'd scald for me to drink in the mornings. I didn't think about the significance of dates, moon cycles and dark nights to the cultivation of yam, but I understood even then that hers was a technical and intimate knowledge of *grung tings* and, more specifically, an intimate knowledge of yam. Yes, intimacy was how I thought of it: I was born into a world where the connection between people and their food, and the ground that produced it, was one of lavish care and intimacy. The feeling I had then – I can't explain why – was that people spoke to the ground. Mama's runic mutterings gave to the yams – afu, mozella, Sinvinsen, barby, taw – a kind of mystique. Even now I think of yam as a mystery food.

At midday, the men would prepare a communal pot of stew peas, featuring salted beef or pig's tail, yam, dasheen, coco and boiled plantain. The smoke would go up through the yam vines and into the mango tree, and I'd be alongside Mama and all the other adults, savouring the camaraderie. The break lasted until two o'clock, and the men spent it resting or sleeping in the shade of the trees or sharpening their cutlasses. When the times for harvesting the yams arrived and the harvest was big, Mama would get a man from the village to help her. However, it was usually just Mama and me occupying this plot of land. Yes, yam planting was considered 'men's work', though it never struck me as odd that Mama did most of it on her own. Sometimes a friend – Maas Amos or someone else from the church – would come to transport the yams back to our home; otherwise, she would borrow someone's donkey. Mama did the weeding, the mulching and the tending of the vines. She knew the work as well as any of the men; there were few things she didn't do.

She was only a small woman, Mama, barely over five feet, but with strong calves. Her voice would easily become shrill; it was her way of compensating for its pitch, a treble that might otherwise be associated with meekness. Her frame – small but strong. Her look – hardy and determined, but also careful and tended. Red dirt smearing her colourful frocks, encrusting the backs of her hands during the week; trimmed fingernails, oiled, supple skin and two neat pigtails to go to church on Sunday. A mouth that was often pouting. Doing jobs reserved for men (planting yams, digging), she was

Portrait of Mama taken at a studio in Kingston in the mid-1960s.

what the country people termed a 'bad woman', but she clothed this in piety. Whatever her reasons, she was tied to her church.

I would spend a whole day there at the grung. One whole day by myself around the mango tree, never roaming into other yam fields or into the woodland. Just there, playing with beetles, rocks and the seeds of mangoes, while Mama worked. In those days, I watched and dreamed. Imagined myself going up in a helicopter like the toy one my cousin, Sister Vads, sent me from New York. I dreamed of being a preacher and preached to myself and the trees and the grass. I ate common mangoes and grew tired of them. Did I know the concept of 'getting bored'? This unhurried rhythm was ingrained in daily life. It was in this way that I learned to love silence; to listen to the languages of other things, like hoes, like cutlasses. It grew into watching the vines until I could hear them, for if you watch anything long enough you will hear it – the chlorophyll being distilled in the stalks and moving; the gaulins' cry and the cows. The grung music, the grung life.

It's July 2022. The first time I'm able to fly since the spate of lockdowns. Here I am in my hillside district. And, really, though she's long dead, I'm here to find Mama. Naturally, the path to her leads through the grung. It's been decades since I last stood on that nameless hill leading to it. I see the scattered rocks, some round, some pointed, that we try to avoid in order not to buck our toes. How far Mama had to walk to get to her grung! The land that she leased from Lascelles and Edith, her 'church brethren'. Had it always been so far away? Had the hill always been so steep? The tall guango tree is no longer there. Would it look as big and imposing to me now?

A house – plastered but unpainted, with a concrete roof deck and wooden windowpanes – now occupies the space where the tree once rose and spread. Here, where there once was a clearing shaded by a towering guango, a housing settlement. I don't know the names of the families whose houses line each side of the dirt track. Yet, from where I stand, overlooking the expanse of land Mama once tended, its contours evoke a sense of recognition. And there, amidst the terrain, stands the familiar silhouette of the mango tree.

Now there are two neat fences separating Mama's old grung from the rest of the land. To the left, Terrence, born to Lascelles and Edith, has constructed his home – a symbol of his rootedness in this soil. Perhaps all the new structures I glimpse belong to this family, kin near and distant. On the right side of the fence, fresh faces have claimed their stake. Inheritances, passings, the dawn of new bloodlines. Fences and borders, rarely seen here when I was a child, are features, now, of the landscape. Yet, amidst this evolution, the land before which I stand still bears an intense familiarity. The big mango tree, my favourite place, is on the outer side of the fence, on the land that Terrence now occupies, cleaved away from our grung, which is now covered with tomatoes, a bed stretching to where the land crests, a hump beyond which I cannot see.

It seems to me that, in a family, the more room there is to think – the greater the space for self-reflection – the more speech there is. The freedom to express one's creativity often paves the way for vibrant discourse. Yet, when I take inventory of the grung and of our home, where not speaking was the natural order, a line from Annie Ernaux comes to me: 'In our milieu, nothing was thought, everything was

9

accomplished.' Didn't my creativity develop in those years? Surely it did. My imagination evolved in the narrow spaces in which I thrived, communicating differently, in the grung, under a mango tree. There were few books in our home and not much of a culture around their use. How did I become a person of words, of poetry? I can only conclude that in that silence and the way I filled it, in the way I created narrow spaces for myself in the outdoors, there was already something of the poetic. Ever since, I've been on a long, arduous journey to translate the wonder of the grung into language.

Conveying the beauty of an environment not typically considered beautiful is a process akin to translation – getting yourself to hear, see and feel, on its own terms, a landscape merely linked to destitution; it's a demanding endeavour. More than that, acknowledging that my creative impulse originates in this setting has been an essential journey of its own.

In my mind, there's a close relationship between language and landscape. Both are imaginary, yet physical. I believe that language engages one's sense of space; each language suggests a different way of taking up space in the world. Language is place, is flesh. I can feel its thickness as I sink into it. Within this Jamaican English of mine there's the grung and there's Coffee Grove.

So, here I am again in the middle of Mama's grung, taking inventory of the space. Mama putting her cotta on her head in order to lift up her basket and balance it there as we walk to the grung. Memory of the red earth, the association of this redness with abundance itself; the shade from the mango tree. A sadness about all I can't remember. Wondering how to channel everything from that time into me, yet knowing everything is already here *inside* me. A difficult happiness – tinged with the harshness of our aloneness. The difficulty of separating one emotion from the other. The sadness of seeing her work all alone, of realising that she did not complain, at least not nearly as much as she was entitled to. Memory of watching her while watching the earth teem with vines, shoots, suckers, ants, beetles, things being formed out of wood and mulch. Biding my time, enjoying the tranquillity that Mama paid for. There was *a language* in which 'we had little', a language of class and fate and money; only later did I encounter it. For now, there was the abundance of the earth, of her crops, of our food, a satisfaction that words cannot describe. That sadness and that confidence form my character, its attention to the ground, its love of plants and living things, its love of the trees.

Leeds, England. January 2019. My family and I move to a neighbourhood here named Roundhay. It's home to Roundhay Park, one of the largest parks in Europe. This move is a turning point in my life. Suddenly, with 700-plus acres of park and woodland on my doorstep, all sorts of questions arise in my mind. The change in my social class is evident. Before my eyes, all this green space, and along with it the possibility of 'going for walks' – long walks – something I've never done before, but which I can start doing now because my job affords me time in the middle of the day. People who 'go walking' don't even realise that it's a socially coded practice. All of a sudden, I'm noticing what was unavailable to me before, in Britain, the country I migrated to in search of a 'brighter future' a decade ago, arriving with my scholarship to pursue graduate studies at Oxford University. In

Roundhay, I realise that I've made it. I've become the person I'd been dreaming of. But what does that mean, in the end? I'm now going walking – how funny! – but it's taken a change of class to realise that my life of social climbing has in fact been one of privation all these years. I've been alienated from land, from planting, from watching things grow. Because of the realities attached to my socio-economic background and, to a certain degree, my skin colour, the possibilities of connecting with nature upon arrival in Britain have been slimmer. They're available to some degree, but the realities of class also made me take longer to be aware of them, to search them out.

This realisation makes me angry, as I begin to see just how much class keeps people in Britain from the privileges of land and soil and also keeps them from the tenderness that comes with forming kinship with the earth. At the same time, this has led me into a fierce reclamation of that tenderness, which was the purpose of *Thinking with Trees*, the book I started writing more than a year before the first pandemic lockdown. I'm not going to waste any more time. I'm fiercely reclaiming my body's right to slowness, to the 'lavishness' of spending time among trees and growing things.

Ultimately, what moving to Roundhay Park has led me to is a search for my childhood. In Yorkshire, I've come to meet a landscape I saw all the time as a child, through my education, in the books we were made to study at school: daffodils, squirrels, the heather, the moor. And I feel the sadness coming on again. Sad about having had to live in another person's landscape, about thinking that their landscape was better than mine, about desiring their landscape more than I desired my own. For me, the only logical result of this awakening is to immerse myself once again in the memories of the verdant hills of Coffee Grove, Jamaica. I'm also here because of a landscape that I have constructed. The bridge between Coffee Grove, with its yam fields and farmlands, and Oxford, with its dreaming spires, between peasant me and current me going for walks in a park in Leeds, runs right through Mama.

As I go walking in the park, the green pulls at something inside me. The enormous, muscular beech reminds me of the unclimbable guango. Trees, barks, plants, mushrooms, leaves, bird calls. It's all very different, of course. I do not know the names of flowers here and have only just learned to identify a few of these trees. I stroll through the woods with an app on my phone, whipping it out at the site of a curious-looking one whose shape fascinates me – a fern-leaved beech, a blue Atlas cedar, a towering black pine. I'm fascinated by the patterns of the barks, their complex textures.

My mind goes back to my first spring in the flat in Roundhay Park. In May, as flowers suddenly appeared from a landscape of grey metal, and trees slowly created magical canopies and bowers, I summoned my app to tell me who these creatures were. I can hardly think about it now without referring to V. S. Naipaul and his novel *The Enigma of Arrival*, which I read a couple of years after that moment. In that novel, Naipaul uses a term I'll never forget: 'my second life of seeing'. That expression captures so well the experience I began to have when I moved to Roundhay Park. It's as if all the ways of walking and of looking at trees, shrubs and plants that I had developed as a child in Coffee Grove, and which had been suppressed with the years, awakened themselves again to me. I was having a childhood all over again. All the urges of touching and speaking to trees, of connecting my desires to plants, of hearing everything that would speak to me in the silence, were alive again.

But the beings among whom I walked, the myriad flowers of that first spring, the mysterious trees with their complex foreign barks, were opaque to me. All I was privy to was the denseness and richness of their unknown lives and identities. The sense of the unavailable was a gift, more powerful and open than if I'd been native to this landscape and had known all their names. Because I was a child again. To be a child is to feel intensely and yet to be estranged. In the childhood gaze, wonder thrives, and wonder is the source of joy. Being a child was saving me, freeing me, loosening me.

In the hillside village of Coffee Grove, Jamaica, I didn't know the riches I had. I did not know that, thirty years later, I would hunger for the spunk of chlorophyll in chocho and yam vines. For rain battering zinc roofs, for games in the bush, in the roots of the cotton tree. But right now, I'm here, standing, taking my time, owning space. My transformation has not only changed my future, it has also changed my past.

I am stepping into tenderness. This tenderness – the delicate touch of plants, the warmth of being embraced by their world, the earth's sensuality – might have been there before, but I was never able to see it. I was too blinkered, too focused on my life of social climbing. Besides, my sphere was the urban: I had never imagined myself close to the earth; among plants, trees and green life, in a place like England. I had never once visualised my body within its forests and wild places. So this 'tenderness' was always there and yet invisible to me. What's allowed me to finally perceive it? It's our current times, marked by the resurgence of anti-Black sentiment. My electronic devices offer me a steady supply of this violence. It reaches me at unsuspecting hours on Instagram and X – digital content, everywhere. It's the horrifying images seared into my mind: the sight of a police officer kneeling on the neck of George Floyd in Minneapolis, the scene from Paris of a policeman shooting the teenage Nahel at point-blank range. The documented brutality against protestors amplifies the anguish. It's the plight of elderly West Indians, who answered Britain's call to rebuild after the Second World War, now facing expulsion in their twilight years. It's the palpable surge of hostility towards the Black community in various quarters of England, driven by a sense of resentment over their integration into society – a sentiment encapsulated by the politics of a 'hostile environment' and amplified by echoes of Enoch Powell's rhetoric of replacement conspiracies.

This general reset of anti-Blackness, which would have prominent political leaders embracing, even promoting, police brutality against Black bodies, has thrust into stark relief the need for tenderness, my need to reclaim it. How do Black people find tenderness while being threatened in the world? How do we find tenderness while fighting to preserve our bodies? This is what this journey is about. The possibility of tenderness: the escape from the rage in which racism endeavours to confine me. More than a desire, it's an insistence on tenderness. This is enough in itself. But I can't seem to separate this urge towards tenderness from the joy and release that I find in the world of plants, in the sensuality of having my hands in the soil, in the joy of seeing things grow. There's an impulse of life in these things that's irrepressible, and in this impulse that draws me to the soil, I find ways of living through – if not beyond – the constraints of racism. The plants I speak about, the people I portrait, the stories I tell about the land, are my ways into describing a new form of living while Black in a country like Britain.

Anger? Of course. But also, what about the empowering force of non-anger? Yes, this book arises out of anger; anger hovers all around it, even though, on the surface, it seems to sidestep this theme. But why? Because we need the space to not be angry. Beautiful expressions of rage can be inspiring and empowering. That said, this book arises out of a particular impulse: the right to non-anger. The right to have time to not be angry. The right to have time not *marked* by anger. Perhaps it might be a question that I'm trying to answer here: If anger can be productive, why do I insist on the right for my writing not to proceed from it? Why do I seek a space of thinking, of being, that does not flow from it? Why do I want to write a book in which it is not the weather, the unspoken weather? My response: I'm wary of racism's theft of time. By inciting us to anger, the system achieves just that: the pillaging of time. It robs us of the moments where we shape our narratives according to our own desires, our own dreams and the legacies of our ancestors. The result: we're trapped in reaction time, with all the impacts this has on our health and well-being. The possibility of tenderness is the possibility of a form of living governed by the sovereignty of our own time: by the ability to have rest, to slide away from a racist system that incites us to constantly respond to it. The possibility of our hands in the soil, among the plants, in the land. The possibility of experiencing the tactile joy and sensuality of nurturing life. I'm looking for a world where I can shift my focus from my epidermis, bringing my earth-hood into focus.

Here, then, is Coffee Grove. Here's the grung; here, the journey. Here, the possibility of tenderness.

*. . . the way my heartbeat raced as I began to see that world
form, as I began to feel new meaning flow beneath my skin . . .*

*Your eyes allow you to see the terrain before you, to commit a
familiar room to memory, but there's a sixth sense that renders
a place familiar.*

It's in the tongue.

The tongue, too, is a means of taking up space,

a way for the world to enter you.

The tongue to give place

to existence.

The tongue to turn

sub-characters

into main plot.

2.

A People's History of the Land

Dawn is always rhythmic and sure: a steady growing of the light that happens over one hour, from the moment those first wan sunrays begin to creep in to the moment you clearly see the dew on the grass. The roosters have quieted their crowing. Six o'clock, and the neighbours are already up and moving, getting their little boy ready for school. From the veranda, I watch the day's early choreography through the lattice of the burglar bars. From the nearby woodland, a symphony of birdsong, prompting me to strain my ear for familiar melodies. As the clock inches towards seven, my neighbours leave in their car, and with my trusty cafetière brimming with coffee, I move to the broad table in the dining section of my large, unpartitioned room, where I sit to write every day. First thing in the morning – get it all out, remember and process all the happenings of the previous day, before taking your phone off airplane mode, before turning on the Wi-Fi button on your computer.

This morning, after an intense four-hour writing session, I get ready to leave the house. I wait for my mother to arrive from Mandeville, meeting me at the place I'm currently occupying, a house provided by Miss Rita, a friend of hers residing overseas. I want to convince Mommy to accompany me on a journey to Mount Pleasant. My destination? Faranuff, a woodland settlement located within the district.

It's one of my mother's childhood haunts. The name resonates with poetic allure, stirring a fascination that matches
my eagerness to lay eyes upon the place.

Mommy pulls her worn sedan into the front yard of Miss
Rita's. Amid greetings, she slips into the passenger seat of
my car and we set off along the Coffee Grove road, arriving
at Mount Pleasant in around ten minutes. At the entrance to
the village, I can't help but notice the old but robust foundations of a ruined house and am intrigued by the stonemasonry,
which is obviously from a very different time. *Is what kind o'
building yuh think used to be up de-so?* I ask, slowing down. We
park the car below the steep hillside at the top of which the
stone foundations are perched, at the edge of an abrupt
incline. To get a closer look, we leave the main road. A
narrow track allows us access to the portion of land invisible
to us from below; we follow it. What's before our eyes
evokes the ruins of some ancient world. At first, it appears,
simply, as an infinity of rocks, many of which have been
heaped into cairn-like mounds. The piling of rocks is a ritual
performed by those who toil the land, driven by a blend of
practicality and perhaps something more profound. While
farmers seek to optimise arable space amidst rocky terrain,
could these stone stacks also serve as ancient storytellers?
Are they silent symbols of human connections etched into
the very earth?

It's obvious that the ground on which we're walking was
once under the ocean. The karst limestone geology, forged
over millennia, bears witness to Jamaica's emergence from
the seas some fifteen million years ago. Just like in Coffee
Grove, the karst is so oceanic in Mount Pleasant that it sometimes seems like ocean waves have only just receded, revealing

white limestone rock in jumbled formations. Paths are rocky, and the craggy limestone might seem hostile to some; it's the very opposite of smooth. Both Mount Pleasant and Coffee Grove are predominantly formed of this limestone. Caves, sinkholes and underground passages abound.

People farm this prohibitive ground of rocks and sink-holes. I can see a lone pumpkin on its vine, almost invisible among the jumble of boulders. A number of other vines can be seen running among the crags, and when you look care-fully, paths begin to appear, walkways; beneath the rockiness, you begin to see an organised, tended landscape.

Soon, if your eye lingers, you even notice a superimpos-ition of landscapes. In one way, this seems an ancient, prehistoric world. There's something humbling about the vista: you sense in the giant rocks the presence of a very large timescale. This spread of stones and standing boulders is dramatic. From another gaze, it's just a peasant grung, serving the needs of families and generating a small income.

Further down the track, Mommy and I observe the old stonework foundations. They're from a sizeable house whose walls were probably made of earth and stone. They're the foundations we noticed from the main road, but from this perspective, they're almost something entirely different. There's a kind of aliveness to the place that we couldn't have imagined from down in the street, as if there were some-thing ongoing about it.

It's here, in this district of Mount Pleasant, that my grand-mother first lived when she arrived in the area, at the end of a five-year flight away from her family in St Elizabeth. In a house that once stood around a kilometre away from our current location at the edge of the village, she settled here after marrying Brother Joe, my grandfather. There, in that house, thirteen years later, she had my mother, Miriam, to whom they gave the pet name Dwina.

Dwina and I stand looking at the earth and the landscape, thinking about the layers of time that include us while transcending us by far. Amidst our musings, she shares a captivating anecdote about a boy called Eulie, from the generation preceding her own. It's a story that became a sort of legend in the district. One day, Eulie disappeared and his parents, sick with fear, sounded the alarm. A search was launched. Some villagers eventually found him on the edge of the famed sinkhole that has no name, the one located in the thicket of woodland just beyond the depression we're now looking at. It's somewhere near the stream whose water we can hear from up here. The hole is bottomless. It's where the villagers carry dead cows to dispose of them. The carcasses fall in without a sound, the hole yielding no smell.

Legend has it that if you cast a stone into this abyss, you'll find it again in Porus, a town lying deep at the foot of the mountain. I often heard people say that Porus had eight rivers running under it. Stories of the world beneath us – of what lies or might lie under our feet – exert a special kind of fascination on me. I find it extraordinary, almost magical, to think that much of the river where my playmates and I used to bathe in Porus was situated underground.

The boy Eulie squatted at the edge of this sinkhole, unsuspecting of danger, stringing together pieces of wiss – as we, here, call lianas. He extended his plumb line of wisses further and further into the depths, each new addition bringing him closer to touching the bottom of the hole. Four years old is the age of wonder, of discovery of a world still enveloped in mystery. I can imagine our four-year-old daughter, Leyla, discovering this sinkhole, where a rock thrown in makes no sound. I can see her doing the same sort of thing as Eulie.

Of course, the boy would never touch the bottom of the hole, and thankfully, the villagers found him there, alive. As I listen to Mommy's anecdote, certain connections begin to form, not unlike the underground network of streams said to be running beneath our feet. In the earliest known account detailing Jamaica's geology, penned by Henry Thomas De la Beche in 1826, he vividly describes the island's white lime-stone formation as riddled with countless holes and caverns, where the waters mysteriously vanish. This narrative is all the more intriguing given De la Beche's own background as a slaveholder. Inheriting sugar plantations in Clarendon at the tender age of twenty-one, he became part of a world whose economic concerns were intertwined with explor-ation and mappings of various kinds, where geological maps became the means for making land visible for colonial extraction – in a word, where mapping became a capitalist exercise.

The specific catalyst behind De la Beche's journey to Jamaica is truly fascinating. Faced with dwindling profits due to frequent slave uprisings, he embarked on a research exped-ition to the island between 1823 and 1824, aiming to map its geological features. Providing the planter class with a detailed understanding of the island's topography – replete with numerous hiding spots for escapees from the plantation – De la Beche could help stem the financial fallout from fugitive slaves. His research sought insights into one of the mechan-isms facilitating slave revolts: a cavern-filled, mountainous geology that seemed to come to the aid of runaways and facilitated the planning and execution of attacks and raids.

Who would have imagined that the first official geological research into Jamaica was spurred by financial motives? It's a testament to the intricate web of connections that shape our history, revealing unexpected intersections between profit, power and the knowledge we take for granted today.

Writing about my region well over a hundred years later, the Latvian geologist Verners Zans notes:

> This is a rugged topography, formed by numerous deep dolines (cockpits), collapse structures, sinkholes and solution cavities of various kinds, between which conical or tower-shaped hills rise to several hundred feet . . . The limestone rock is very cavernous, penetrated by numerous cavities, subterranean conduits and caves, some of which are traceable for miles.

Says my mother: *I've often been told that there are caves in Mount Pleasant.* These caves, like the sinkhole of village fame, are hidden in plain sight, shielded by legend as much as by the thick vegetation of the woodlands into which – according to many – one must not venture. Alan Fincham's *Jamaica Underground* lists both caves and sinkholes that are near to where we currently are – near and yet far, as things do often feel in this landscape of high peaks, steep hills, ravines, gullies. These include the Peace River and Victoria Caves; the two districts they are named for are known to my mother mostly through stories. They are virtually unknown to me. The journey by car might be only around six or seven miles from Mount Pleasant, but it's along very sinuous and, as always in the country, bad roads, full of mini sinkholes themselves! The journey by foot, taking us through the forest, is perhaps only two miles long, but the path presents so many obstacles that it might take the uninitiated an hour or more to get there. This is the land my family have walked. I begin to imagine stories of fugitive slaves hiding out in underground caves, finding subterranean pathways unknown to their European captors, the self-declared 'settlers' of this island. I've heard several such stories or read them in books while at school.

Then no muss? Where you think them Maroon people-de used to hide? Whole heap a hiding place up-ya, declares my mother, responding to my thoughts voiced out loud. My thoughts naturally drift to De la Beche mapping the island's underground geology, spurred by the profit margin.

As it happens, the geology of this location is inseparable from its history as a coffee-growing district in the slavery plantation era, and, consequently, from its inscription within a larger, global history. Unexpectedly, it's this visit to Mount Pleasant that has me making the connection between coffee growing, slavery, Britain and Coffee Grove. Mount Pleasant's and Coffee Grove's geological structure must have been hugely significant to the coffee estates that existed here in the eighteenth and nineteenth centuries. The underground rivers and streams that run below it emerge as water courses that provided power to the coffee mills of this area. The river here, which people simply refer to as Dam Head River, is a case in point. It powered the mills of the Whitney Plantation, a large coffee-growing estate that neighboured Mount Pleasant. In fact, the dam from which the river derives its name was built for that purpose. It must also have been precious to the Coffee Grove Estate, I muse, as this type of water supply was essential for the various functions of the estate – the washing of coffee beans, the provision of drinking water for cattle and horses, etc.

It dawns on me that alongside this exploitable source of water power, the rolling hills that Mommy and I see all around us were perfect for the soil drainage that coffee needs. Not only is mountainous Manchester one of the best areas in the country for the cultivation of coffee, but the coffee grown here is comparable in quality to that of the famed Blue Mountains.

It would be true to say that the coffee bean connects this world of Mount Pleasant and Coffee Grove to England, the world I now inhabit. Within the tapestry of global coffee history, these Jamaican villages emerge as poignant threads. The cultivation of coffee on the Coffee Grove Estate in the eighteenth and nineteenth centuries has everything to do with the emergence of the coffee house as a phenomenon in London during this time. Recently, at the British Library, I came across the *West India Committee Circular* of 16 July 1925. It noted that agents of the colonies 'not unnaturally found the taverns and coffee houses of the period [mid-seventeenth century to 1864] suitable places in which to meet to discuss affairs and draft letters'. In this period, it further remarked, many a professional man adopted a coffee house as his permanent address. By 1864, when stamp and paper duties had been abolished, the coffee houses had laid the foundation of the modern club. Simultaneously, I can't ignore the stark reality that the rise of coffee consumption as a bourgeois trend in Europe is inextricably tied to the brutal history of slavery.

Pressed with these questions, I want to share them with the writer and scholar Erna Brodber, with whom I've started a correspondence. Dr Brodber, a sociologist, is nothing less than a Jamaican national treasure – a formidable intellectual and one of my favourite writers (she's also a novelist). She's famous for exploring in her work the kinds of questions I'm now asking – around land, Afro-Jamaican inheritance, the construction of society in peasant Jamaica. Luckily, I'll be seeing her tomorrow. Hearing my initial questions about land in Coffee Grove, not only has she pointed me to the National Land Agency – something I didn't even know existed – she's suggested we go together.

Right now, though, Mommy and I re-emerge from the track that led us through the rocky field to the old stone foundations. Coming out, we pass alongside Maas Owen's home. He's one of Mama's comrades – the dirt track in fact belongs to him, and so does a part of the field. Skirting the wall of the house, we're back on the Mount Pleasant main road and can see Maas Owen on his veranda, and Mr Lee, his drinking partner, sitting beside him. Crying *howdy* from the street, we unlatch the wooden gate and walk up to them, exchanging the greetings of friends – almost clan people – who haven't seen each other in ages. At the same time, we fall in as if we were picking up a conversation paused yesterday. It's a weird combination of long distance and deep familiarity, with words flying here and there about *how you turn big, big man now*; and also *how you look responsible*; and *Dwina, you must so proud . . . You must so happy fi see him . . . Can you imagine, likkle Tommy turn big man so . . . Bwoy, Sister Morgan* [Mama] *must happy. . . .* I nod and smile in respect to the elders. Sister Morgan was how most people here referred to Mama.

Him want to go see Faranuff, Mommy announces to Maas Owen and Mr Lee. It's not 8 a.m. yet, but they've been on the rum already; I can smell it on their breath. They often meet up in this house, which Maas Owen has occupied alone ever since his wife left to go live overseas. *Eh-eh, eh-eh.* Maas Owen is tickled. He nods his lively eighty-year-old head, his happy demeanour having something to do with, I think, his early-morning whites. *A old time something dem-deh Tommy.* Those days won't come back again, he says to me. But he's excited about the book I'm writing, and that it's about the land in Mount Pleasant and Coffee Grove. I'm surprised at how enthusiastic both he and Mr Lee are, asking all sorts of questions: about when the book will come out, about who's in it, and what I talk about. We chit-chat about various happenings in the district, and after giving us a large, ripe avocado to go along with our bulla cakes, Maas Owen decides that we should get up off his veranda wall and get back on the road. Good-naturedly, we comply, leaving the car parked where we first stopped. Mommy leads the way and soon enough we reach her childhood home. It sits on lands she still owns, lands bequeathed to her by Joe Morgan, her late father.

The land lies at a fork in the road, the right side of the fork being the Mount Pleasant Road, which winds its way up to Garlogie, Banana Ground and further into the parish of Clarendon, and the left side, the dusty track that leads into the tiny settlement of families which once included Mommy's. As we stand in the dusty track, Mommy points to the boundaries of her property, which encompasses a portion of the former site of the Morgan family home where my mother was born. It then extends upwards, over a mini wilderness, a thicket of trees and bramble that seems quite impassable. Behind this mini wilderness, at the top of a hill, is a piece of land I presume is cleared for the purposes of cultivation. I've never seen it, nor can I see it from where we now stand in the dirt track, but it adjoins properties that Joe, my grandfather, sold off to other families, including a man named Tony Codner. In addition to his own, Codner now cultivates Mommy's parcel of land; he's 'leased' it from her, meaning that some twenty years ago, Codner paid my mother – fifty dollars – as a mere gesture. The most important condition of the 'lease' is that periodically Codner should give Mommy a portion of the yields of the land, which is to say, the agreement is bound by a huge dose of good faith and a regular provision of yams. People just trust each other to do the right thing.

Standing here beside Mommy's piece of earth, hearing the account of sizes and boundaries, and of purchases, reminds me that my grandfather Joe had owned a huge amount of land. This is something I'd forgotten, especially since Daddy Joe has never occupied a prominent place in the story I've been able to put together about my family. That his family – I've heard the name of his mother, Ma Minky, but nothing of his father – were among the peasants who came into substantial amounts of land in this district from the early twentieth century is certain. What stories have been buried with him! What stories have failed to be transmitted because people here don't talk about the past, don't consider it something worthy of discussing.

I do remember that when Daddy Joe died and left this bump of land to Mommy – back then, I couldn't have gauged the significance of two and a half acres – my mother complained bitterly that he'd disinherited her. I was eight or nine at the time. When she wept – after hearing of his death – I remember thinking it was on account of her 'disinheritance'.

Like the vast majority of peasants in this area, all my mother has now is a common-law title, based on her father's will saying he'd bequeathed this patch to her. She has that, and the diagram of the property. She's convinced that this protects her interests, despite my repeated insistence that she apply for a registered title. For that, there's paperwork involved – something about the owners of the adjoining properties 'swearing off' their boundaries – and lots of money.

The place is jagged, Mommy says, *because my daddy sell it funny. Cut it up piece a-piece a, rather than follow any sensible order.*

Daddy Joe would sell a little bit here and there when he needed money. *Sell it to Norell, Tony, John Brown, Leroy Wilson, Tat-dem, Siri . . .* I don't remember any of these people. I tell Mommy she may have to negotiate with the other parties to buy back some of their land to improve the quality of her holding. Her answer: a deviation, as happens when she can't imagine herself in a position that should or could have been hers by right.

Me always tell Tony fi buy it, you know, I say Tony, you live there, why not buy the land from me so that you have your own walkway into your yard?

> *A you fi a buy from him*, I retort, *that's how we have to be thinking now.* We're the ones who're supposed to be buying up land. *Land a the most expensive thing on this earth*, I add, attempting to sound wise.

Mi aunty, Miss Gatha, she a the one we bury ya-so. And some of her likkle pickney them did bury here as well. She points to a burial plot that has small tombs. *Miss Gatha baby them what dead.* Miss Gatha being my grandfather's sister, who conceived sixteen children, dying in childbirth from the sixteenth one. *Over ya-so,* Mommy proceeds, *is Sister Vads' land.* Sister Vads: one of Miss Gatha's daughters, the lady who sent me the toy helicopter from New York, the one I imagined going up in the air in, in the games of pretend I played under the mango tree at Mama's grung. My mother is giving me something of a family grounding in this settlement, as in, *you may as well come know your roots.*

All of over ya-so used to be fi we. The entire lane. *And this is where Daddy Joe sisters-them bury.* A voyage into the 'origins' of our family. How important this is, how significant to see your connections to the soil – to touch it, so that your history becomes physical. It's a kind of mapping, too. Certainly, Mommy is mapping her childhood, talking about a man called Jim Thompson, the only one to have a truck in Mount Pleasant when my mother was a child – people depended on him to carry the sick to hospital, to transport produce to market. Among other things, Mama depended on him to carry Mommy to her high school graduation.

Where we turned, Mommy says, her memory suddenly ignited, *there was a shop right de-so, we actually turned into the gateway, an upstairs place . . . that was Jim Thompson's house. He was a rich man, they had upstairs house, and a shop. Him wife was a teacher. Round here,* [pointing to a stretch of uncultivated woodland], *is fi them too . . . Jim Thompson did have one sister, and everybody talk say a the biggest woman that they ever see!*

Oh, the woman whose house wall the man-dem had to knock down to take her body out when she dead? I'm already familiar with this story of the woman whose coffin the pallbearers had to carry using ropes.

When you go round that corner there, past that woodland – she points to a bend in the track as we veer off to the left – *that's Nancy Pond.*

I heard this name all the time as a child in the stories my mother told. Nancy Pond is a place she went to often, a place around which she played. It's part of the geography of her childhood. There is magic in the name Nancy Pond. I've always been hungry for the story behind the name, for projecting myself into those childhood stories of insouciant play. My mother's face would light up and her voice would get brighter when she told them. Those are her best memories. There was a familiarity with the land in the way she said *Nancy Pond*, a sense of place shared among people. Her tales recreated the place right before her eyes. I have always wanted to visit Nancy Pond. And yet, despite its apparent proximity to Coffee Grove and its location near the postal agency in Mount Pleasant where Mama took me daily during the working week, Nancy Pond remained strangely inaccessible to me. If it was her place of joy, why did my mother never take me there herself? Was she afraid of what that joy would awaken? My people are folks who believe that if good moments happened, you'd better leave them where they were. Was there a fear of the emotions that would resurface through the reliving of memories? My folks are a people of silence and willed forgetting. There's no explanation for why we didn't go to Nancy Pond. No explanation for the fact that my mother never took me to her childhood home.

I was thirty-seven years old when I had my first glimpse of this home. I'd come back on vacation from Leeds. It took going to live in England for me to see the land on which my mother was born and on which she grew up. Years of travelling, then, all over the world, and a life built far away from home, for me to finally visit this place, a ten-minute drive away from Coffee Grove. For so much of my life, it was a place almost unreachable. It would have been very possible for my grandmother to take me there in the days when I lived with her, but she had an aversion to the place, was unable to bring herself back there. I didn't realise it then, but there was a wall between her and that old home that was insurmountable, and that wall was all the history between her and Daddy Joe, a history of hurt, separation and loss; one of shame and of the unspeakable; of muteness. A pervasive sense of hurt encapsulating her existence was epitomised by the invisible wall that separated her from the land in Mount Pleasant, despite her role as the postal agent within the district. The site of the former house was just a walk away, but this stone's-throw distance seemed for her a distance of continents; she made it so.

I did wonder, back in the day, why she didn't venture there. I wondered, silent, about many things, since asking questions wasn't allowed. I had been raised, in our world, to know that children didn't have the right to ask questions; that things unsaid were better left unsaid; that it was devious, scheming, ungrateful to want to know the details of big people's lives and their doings. I had been raised to think that to know the story of Daddy Joe and Mama was a disrespect to my elders. There were so many silences in my world.

There's something about the water – about Nancy Pond, about Dam Head – and the centrality of water in the community's life. It may simply speak to how people lived back then. Water was a resource that was shared. People would have to go and fetch it from certain places, and so those places played a significant role in the life of the community. They became meeting points. People depended on them. They were significant points on one's inner map of place, and those places open up like flowers in my imagination; they bloom with the musicality of their names. They seem important to who I am, though I hardly know them. In fact, to date, of all the places of water, I've only been to Dam Head, and that only a few years ago, having known it solely as a place inhabited by my mother's stories. But the names symbolise something atavistic, perhaps something I can't get a hold of. An idea of speech, of language, of sound. A deep intuition about the land, about the body, about how we make lives and how we move.

It's the way places are named after people, as well: Nancy Pond. The way the names carry undocumented stories. It's the absence of a record that intrigues me, the idea that I cannot, and perhaps will never, know the meaning behind Nancy Pond. Perhaps we didn't have the possibility of recording that history. It's all oral storytelling within the peasantry. Perhaps that history, transmitted orally for a long time, somehow escaped us. I'm fascinated by all the histories that escape us. To narrate the tales of these lesser-known lands and their minor characters is also, I muse, an attempt to compensate for these lost histories, or at least a gesture of recognition towards them.

See it ya! Mommy announces, swirling her hand in the air, vaguely, as if she were unable to remember the precise co-ordinates, but the place called Faranuff, she is saying, is very broadly speaking here. *So this is it?* I reply. I don't know exactly what I was expecting, but it was definitely something bigger, slightly more dramatic. Instead, what I see is a small clearing with a little patch of tillage – dried pumpkin vines. We're standing in it. Facing us, withdrawn into the bush that surrounds the clearing, is a little house. To our right, a green hole within a curtain of woodland. It seems barely large enough for a pathway, but rather some kind of tunnel you might get sucked into and disappear.

A man is coming from the direction of the house; he greets Mommy: Money Man, a childhood friend of hers. *No road no de fi gu-dung so again you know*: the road no longer exists. *A pure woodland. You can't walk there*, he assures us. The road from Nancy Pond is still passable, he says, but this one has been blocked for years. *You woulda haffi go round pass Auntie Mack them*, he insists, *then go dung side-a John Martin-de*. We enter out of pure dare. As we approach, the chlorophyllic coolness rises towards us and our voices become felted. Money Man joins us for the walk. Faranuff is not a huge place, then; it's almost a non-place. It's just a steep, descending rock track. Who knows, this may be the remnants of a larger place, because 'Faranuff' is also the name given to the woodlands through which this track runs, woodlands in which people once lived. We're seeing the ruins of the houses now, the broken-down walls. Brother Son, Sister Liddy – names I vaguely remember because they were really old when I was a child. *Bush*. It's been years since people stopped using this path, and Money Man is curious as to why we'd want to come here. *Nothing special*, Mommy tells him, *we just want to come and see – just because*.

Sharp, pointed hills and numerous ferns, thick lianas named brial wiss. The flora is dense here with all sorts of plants and wisses that cleanse the body, treat illnesses; with woodland things that people use for myriad healing purposes. There are those who know intimately the hordes and throngs of them, the great company of herbs. Mama was one of these people, the type who would walk through a woodland, down sharp, winding paths like this one, just to find a herb that grows in the cool places – one that has to be searched for, like Jack ina bush, growing in the stony woodlands. I'm taking photos of the tangle, but it's a challenge to take good photos in this space: almost everything is green; it's hard to get contrast. The monotony of my photos belies the richness of what's here. I recognise what I'm convinced is jointa, the plant from the South American kava family, with the spicy aroma that I adored as a child. To treat belly aches, jointa is one of the herbs Mama often gathered. I loved the pungent odour it released upon being broken; I could taste it. Right now, I'm trying to conjure the spicy quality of its smell. But the stem I've snapped doesn't have this familiar aroma, even if Money Man assures me it's the real thing. Our olfactory memory holds remarkable power, and a smell can instantly transport you back to your childhood. My mother guesses that this might be a 'wild jointa', from the same family, but not the one we use to make tea.

You want to turn back? Mommy asks me, wondering out loud whether forcing our way through this tangle might be absurd. *No way.* I want to go the distance, to encounter the physical places of her memories.

As I continue to take photos, Mommy and Money Man, my two guides, trade stories and share memories: Money Man's are about coming down here to shoot birds, mostly woodpeckers and baldpates that he'd carry home to roast – food. Mommy's are about how early she'd have to wake up and how long she'd have to walk this track before reaching the Coffee Grove main road, then to Bellefield, where she'd get a bus to Mandeville; about dark night catching her on the way back; about how terrified she'd be about encountering a duppy.

Them road-ya make your legs strong . . . I strain for something to fill a long silence, as we concentrate on where we place our feet. For my mother, the rocks on this path were, above all, accidents to avoid – a bucked toe or a gash on the leg. For the young teenager who's just started attending secondary school in Mandeville, the big town, keeping her body safe from injuries takes up a big space in her mind, the space that trips to the beach and family holidays might occupy in the minds of her schoolmates, the ones in her class at Manchester High, the grammar school attended by mostly well-off, light-skinned children. She, the bright little girl from Coffee Grove, has passed an exam that granted her a place at this school, which means moving from the local all-age, where all the other kids from Mount Pleasant and Coffee Grove go.

Mommy is looking at ferns, taking pictures of flowers with her smartphone. She's beside herself with excitement at finding a wild pine flower. *As children, we used to use this to make breeze mills*, she reminisces, bending over to look closely at it. My mother shares my fascination for layers of earth, time and history, a fascination which, in her case, manifests itself in the compulsion to have her hands in the soil and, more specifically, in her love of flowers. A part of her delight is being able to share her knowledge about them, and there's something of the teacher in her that resurfaces:

You see this fern here: inna foreign [meaning, the United

37

States and the UK], *they call it baby's breath. Even this mother-in-law tongue* [another watergrass], *people put it into pots in the United States and sell it for a hundred dollars . . .*

You see that? She practically have a PhD in flowers, I jest to Money Man, sparking laughter between us. Mama's love for growing things surely rubbed off on her, but it's the flowers that truly captivate Mommy; she delves into the minutiae that I sometimes fail to see. Presently, her gaze fixates on a cluster of watergrass, a detail most would dismiss. *Look all this watergrass, Money Man*, she exclaims, gesturing towards the verdant patch. *It bloom all blue flowers.* She points out the trilobal petals, hues of blue and violet nestled within the moss-covered stones lining our path.

It good fi prostate problem too, you know, Money Man chimes in from ahead, his voice carrying back to us. He's recounting a tale about a local man who can pee a bit better now that his wife has been brewing him a tea infused with watergrass, soursop leaves and other herbs.

Can you imagine how inna di bush pretty, when the whole of the tree them start to bloom? Mommy remarks as we approach, gesturing towards an ancient poinciana tree adorned with vibrant blossoms. Now she's looking at the ortanique trees and having memories of climbing them; she's admiring all sorts of trees, plants and wildflowers in the woodland: a wild pine growing in an avocado tree, offering drinking water to birds and mongooses; a trumpet tree that has fallen on the poinciana and bonded with it; a broad-leafed liana called *pudding wiss*. Here, the plants, lianas and bushes of the wild woodlands are known and loved. Here, the woodlands are not an obstacle to civilisation, but a place that many people form kinship with. There are paths for donkeys and paths for humans; houses in ruin, overrun with wisses, houses that take you by surprise, like little monsters trying to hide in the bush. Their former inhabitants have died and their children have not replaced them here.

After an hour or so of following the craggy path, during which I keep my head always down so as not to trip on a rock while walking, we get to a level dirt track from which we see banana fields and several houses in the distance, a settlement on the fringes of the woodland. Every new spot we come to elicits fresh memories from Mommy and Money Man around a childhood spent growing up in these bushes – and one anecdote after another about people who've long since died and people who've only recently died. A hundred metres on the flat dirt track might take us ten minutes as they punctuate this memory walk with stops and starts, with moments of storytelling triggered by standing in particular places. For Money Man and Mommy, trading news about the dead is just a way of catching up. People talk a lot about their dead here. Why is talking about the dead a way of bonding among my hillside people? In the way people love to dwell on the lives of the ancestors, bring them into the conversation, you get the sensation that the departed ones are still a part of things. They may avoid confronting unspoken narratives, but invoking the names and stories of the deceased is their way of honouring them:

Then Brother Dan a mi uncle you know – Money Man.

So, you and Neville [my mother's nephew] *a cousin too then . . . !* – my mother, working out family connections.

Boy, everybody up ya-so connected . . . I chime in.

Every other person is related; you can't bad-mouth someone to anyone else, you may be talking about their relative, though people don't display or emphasise their family connections. There's an expectation that you should intuitively know who is related to whom. Because of this, nobody bothers with formal introductions; you're just expected to navigate the intricate web of relationships on your own.

Well, Neville fi call me Auntie you know . . . Mommy continues. *Neville's mother and my older brother a brother and sister by their mother's side.*

And this piece of land here belongs to Champi. That's the pickney that Miss Mary did have with Lecent. That's Money Man speaking.

Miss Mary, you mean Brother Son Mary? . . . *Then mi neva know seh Mary did have pickney with Lecent . . . ?!*

Yes man! The same boy wah did chop off a man hand down a Montego Bay . . . Yasso now, here, this a fi him grung. This is the grung that the said Champi works. *New Years, watchnight, go right inna church go chop off the man hand. Mi think say him did gone a foreign go hide.*

And so the conversation unfolds, weaving together tales of generations past and present – tales of those currently residing in these woodland spaces, as well as those who, despite years abroad, still lay claim to them. In these spaces, tales of triumph and tragedy resonate across time, each adding a new thread to the fabric of local legend.

And seamlessly, Mommy points to a hump of bushes. *See search mi heart deh. Don't you want some of it to carry back to*

England with you? My mother sends me dried search mi heart in the post: that's how essential I find the plant, both for its medicinal properties and for the way it smells and tastes when boiled. Mama drank a lot of it, thinking that it strengthened the heart. That belief is widely held in Jamaica, hence the alternative name of the bush, *strong heart*. The fresh plant is pretty much non-aromatic. *When it smells sweet*, my mommy offers, twirling the bunch of search mi heart to look at its cream-coloured, basket-like flowers, *is when you put it down in the house, the green one, and it slowly starts to dry. Then it give off the most amazing odour.* Seeing a shrub of broad, fat leaves, I exult, certain within myself that this is the real jointa, the one that smells peppery, the unmistakable one. It has whisked me back to my childhood with remarkable clarity. If Proust hailed from these parts, he might have discovered in it a potency reminiscent of his cherished madeleines.

I begin to see the end of our journey approach as we come out of the protective, cocooning woodland and enter a clearing surrounded by a scattering of small houses. A large cistern lies among rocks that point their teeth menacingly upwards in the middle of the clearing, under the tender, suffused light of the late-afternoon sun. I stop to take photos of a jointa bush and of a salindine plant. Despite its striking sonic similarity, I find no connection to celandine, a herb utilised in Britain for treating 'scrofulous diseases'. Our salindine is valued for its floor-cleaning properties. At the end of the journey, another memory activated by standing in the red dirt surrounding the cistern. It's my mother speaking:

When Mass Jeff, a man that used to live on this hillside, did dead, I was likkle and I follow Mama come round here. Them-deh time they didn't have deadhouse or funeral parlour. They went for the ice and put the dead man on it and lay him out somewhere round the back here-so [pointing to an old house in ruins near the cistern], the big ole block of ice . . .

Money Man, chiming in: *The dead had to be buried by five o'clock inna the morning. Fus time* [long ago, when we were kids] *that's how the dead had to be buried. If him dead now* [3 p.m.], *by twelve o'clock tinite them a done the box* [the coffin]. *By five o'clock a morning, two somebody carry him to the hole and bury him. They can't make sun catch him! The body will start to stink.**

So them church him [have his funeral] *the same day?* I enquire.

No, them no have no time fi do that! answers Mommy.

And Money Man quickly adds: *Them deh ne'en deh!* [Those things did not exist back then.] *Because you can't keep the dead more than two day, one day fi make box and one day fi bury him.*

Mommy: *And that time, everybody come out with them saw, and them cutlass, and them tools.*

Today, burials in Jamaica are more like prolonged feasts, with nightly servings of food at the home of the deceased – the *dead yard*, as it's called. For days, there's food and drink for a host of people who've come from far and wide, whether they

---

* In the Patwa we speak in rural areas like Coffee Grove and Mount Pleasant, the third-person subject and object pronouns are *him*, regardless of gender.

knew the deceased well or not. With the singing of the traditional songs associated with 'nine nights', a series of wakes,
and the traditional music of mento bands, now increasingly
mixed with popular dancehall, the person not familiar with
Jamaica might be forgiven for confusing the burial process
with a party.

Money Man's and Mommy's account of a burial contrasts
so much with what we experienced with Mama. I remember now Mommy running around trying to prepare the
dead yard, with the tarpaulin and the nightly feast of curry
goat and mannish water for the people who would cry
shame on us if we said that we couldn't afford it. In those
nine nights of wake and funeral, Mama's last outing, we had
to *take shame out of we yai*, to keep up appearances, so
Mommy got busy with plans. She worked hard to get the
money sorted, the funeral programmes with readings. The
grass was cut at home and the grave dug. And then I, who
had come from the bush to become this Oxford student
living and studying at the grand École normale supérieure
in Paris at the time (my whole life, I've refused to stay in my
place!), needed to *sort out* my plane tickets – meaning, turn
into Anancy, the West African trickster spider, to get the
money to come home.

Returning to the car, we begin our descent back to Coffee
Grove, the wheels tracing the familiar path along winding
roads. In Coffee Grove, it's not long before we're saying
hello to someone Mommy hasn't seen in a while, and a hello
turns into a long conversation and before you know it, we're
out of the car. Now we've stopped at Miss Carmen's shop,
just another spot, another meeting point, along the road.
Miss Carmen's another person I'm supposed to know so

well, given how much she knows about me, but I remember nothing of this warm, middle-aged face looking at me. Carmen, a woman with very dark skin and close-cropped hair, looks to be in her sixties; as the conversation unfolds, I understand that she and my mother *came up together*.

My mother and Miss Carmen exchange greetings. *The house look nice, eh?* says Miss Carmen. Always the house these days when they meet my mother. *Mi so glad se you finally fixing up the house, Dwina,* she continues. *I feel proud and glad yu si, because I was sad that the house just de-de a rotten down and wasp a build nest inna di boxing* [eaves]. *How Sister Morgan must feel happy!*

Everybody's enthusiastic about the renovations that Mommy's doing to Mama's old house. Meanwhile, the man in the corner sitting on the sacks of chicken feed is looking at me and smiling a smile of recognition. And another man comes in for his beer, shaking my hand. Besides Mommy and Miss Carmen, there's a third woman joining the choreography of voices. I can tell from the particular veneer of her skin, the nature of her gaze, the assurance of her smile, that she's a 'foreigner'. There's something that can travel easily, a kind of recognition, which is familiar to me, even though we've never met. Turns out that Elaine has lived in England for many years, having migrated when she was thirteen. Can you recognise a similarity of experience in the way somebody carries their body? In this case, it's two Coffee Grove people living in England. The fact that she migrated there in the late 1960s, as part of the so-called 'Windrush Generation', makes for a major difference in what we've lived, but there are continuities, of course.

There's a whole heap of people gathered outside. A young man comes up to hug Mommy. Mohawk, ankle-length skinny

44

jeans, retro slim-fit tee – everything says hipster, which makes me wager he may be from nearby Porus, but with family in this area. Probably a past student of Mommy's from Porus Primary. There's a bunch of other men whose faces I recognise without being able to remember the story that connects them to me. Always they remember and they're all calling my name. *Tommy, you don't remember me?* There's a young man who looks about my age. He calls me by my pet name: *Tommy, a me haffi carry Tommy pon me shoulder, you know, go a Post Office. Me haffi help Sister Morgan when Tommy too heavy.* I buy a round of drinks for all the men and women standing outside the shop, a dozen people. Hot and cold Guinness, Heineken, Dragon Stout. Everybody is having a drink. I'm sipping a hot Guinness, and it has already started to go to my head.

I'm hungry. And I'm now feeling a kind of euphoria, a mixture of joy and excitement at being here in Coffee Grove again, excitement at actually being here in the village where I grew up; the euphoria of a memory that lives deep in the body – a memory of being in tiny roadside shops like Miss Carmen's. In that dusky intimacy of animal feed, laundry detergent, powdered seasons and ginger bulla cakes. A small, unfussy wooden edifice in which people pull stools close together; where, when thunderstorms break out and they get trapped, listening to the battering of the rain on the zinc roof, people lean into themselves so much that they reveal buried things they wouldn't tell you if they met you on the road. I'm getting drunk on that tribal feeling housed in the body, as the Guinness starts travelling up into my head and the voices of people begin to criss-cross, as the inside of the bar transforms into a verbal rumble.

Up a Johnny – The hilltop, in Mount Pleasant, on which my mother once so clearly heard the roar of the unnamed river in the valley below, she could feel it flowing through her body.

Roun' a Tolloch – The pasture that Mama and I would traverse to get to the postal agency, her place of work.

Roun' a Josiah – An area of Coffee Grove that lies quite off the main road and where my mother's childhood friend, May-May, cultivates a piece of land.

Roun' a Wood – A woodland near my mother's birthplace, named for one Ina Wood, who once lived there.

Tom Hill – A shortcut that joins Coffee Grove to Mount Pleasant, following the course of the unnamed river.

Pinnikle – A high rock in the dense woodlands separating Coffee Grove from Porus. Also, the silent gully below it.

As soon as you know land,
you know it as a story.
You walk among living tales,
place names burnished by
their stories.

You make lists. Hurrying up,
you're anxious. You don't want to forget
the names, don't want to forget to care for the things
that happened but that were not worthy
of story.

3.

Quiet Bonds

Carmen is only slightly older than my mother, Dwina, but unlike her, she chose farming as her vocation and so remained in this district. Her memories of my grandmother have a sharpness that I envy. Hers is the gift of precision, of years of observing her from the outside; whereas my memories of Mama are more like feelings, present in overwhelming urgencies – to stand under the mango tree, to walk up the slope of the grung, to stand at the top of the slope, in the middle of the tomato bed, looking down at the cultivation, to listen to the complex silences of the grung's environment. I'm unable to bring my memories out of my body, to offer them as sentences. My images of her are groanings, sighs, of admiration. They powder away outside my mouth, but inside, they overwhelm me. I wish I could lend to them the articulacy of Carmen's reminiscences. Many of these involve me, but many others are of a time before I was born, the time of my mother. The story of Mama and her grung is the closest I can come to a family saga. How did this little old woman, whom I knew as my grandmother, make herself independent and, through the efforts of herself alone in this faraway district, which she made hers by a mystifying combination of fate and choice, sustain the dreams of my mother and myself, even once we had both turned our backs on this place?

★

These are the questions I pose to Carmen as we converse inside her bar, she positioned in the shadowy space behind the mesh divider, against a towering stack of canned mackerel, I casually leaning against the linoleum-covered counter. Outside, the rumble of laughter and banter persists, with Mommy and Elaine engrossed in their own discussion in one corner, leaving me in this unexpected tête-à-tête. *She neva have nobody*, Carmen states bluntly, which strikes a chord with me. After all, not many women would tend to the land on the scale that Mama did, especially if they had only themselves to rely on. By the time I was born, she'd long been separated from her husband, a man many years her senior, whom some of the older 'brethren' had foisted on her after her conversion and membership of the Church of God in Coffee Grove. It was not uncommon for them to pair off vulnerable young female converts with desperate, withered bachelors.

The circumstances surrounding her departure from Parottee, her native district in St Elizabeth, in 1940, are unknown to us. They had never mattered until recently, meaning that we would never have thought that her leaving Parottee was a result of 'circumstances'. Then a cousin of ours discovered, while searching digitised archives on the internet, a death certificate bearing my grandmother's name and signature. The certificate was for a baby who had died of malaria, a little Norma, six months old. Mama never mentioned this child to anyone, not even to her own daughter, my mother. Piecing back together the story of her life, my mother and I realised it was that very year, the year of the baby's death, that Mama left Parottee and began the peregrinations which would lead her, via Kingston and Clarendon, to this little district of Coffee Grove in Manchester. It is hard to imagine that she had even heard of this district before leaving her ancestral village, so far away, or that she could have conceived of the possibility of living, let alone dying, here. She spent seven decades of her life in this place, far away from any kin. Why? The question is a blank wall at which we stare. Was Mama merely a naïve young woman when she joined the Church of God and married my grandfather, or was she fleeing a thing so large as to render joining the church a reasonable default move?

The conversations in the bar persist with a steady rumble.

A Sister Morgan teach me a school, Elaine reminisces, her voice carrying the weight of nostalgia.

As if offered a springboard, Carmen chimes in. *A Sister Morgan carry my mother go look 'bout her passport fi go a foreign.*

A Sister Morgan teach me fi read. She look 'bout mi brother passport too.

A Sister Morgan get we land title too. All the way a Kingston she go fi sort it. Another voice adds to the chorus of memories.

Mama was like an unpaid, de facto administrator for the village, a sort of mayor.

And what did the people she helped give her for her services? Mommy ponders aloud, her voice tinged with resentment. *A few provisions from their ground?* Most people used to do that as a regular practice, anyway . . .

Mama's marriage to Joe was steeped in the silent yearning for progeny. Thirteen years into their union, my mother emerged as their solitary offspring. Only thanks to a miracle cure was my mother conceived, *for the man did have fault* – so Mama had once revealed to me on her veranda. A year prior to her birth, Keturah – Mama's given name – and Joe had experienced short-lived happiness in the form of a son born at Spalding Hospital. Yet fate dealt a cruel blow, as the infant's life was cut short on the same day, his passing attributed to a tragic mishap during birth. *Mi poor Lloyd Everett . . . Lawd, mi one bwoy . . .* Mama would lament annually, her tears flowing freely for a single day before the tide of grief receded till the following year. Dwina bore witness to this annual ritual. Lloyd's brief life began and ended on 12 May 1958, while my mother entered the world on 29 April 1959, a glimmer of hope amidst the shadows of loss. A decade later, Mama would part ways with Joe, moving down to Coffee Grove with her sole surviving child in tow.

To me, my grandmother's life appears imbued with an uncanny resolve, driving her to construct not just a liveli-hood but a whole universe, entirely on her own. Through Carmen, I learn of the various places she lived after parting ways with her husband in Mount Pleasant, and I trace her path through assorted rented accommodations. *Mount Pleasant – two place, up a one place de-so, out-so a pay rent, then up a Brother Webb, till she fight and buy da place-de* [the house I know today], *and then she build.* The locations echo like stations of an odyssey, a quest for a Promised Land, yet Mama never found what could be deemed a 'promised land' in her lifetime. Each place name, entwined with its own story, paints a picture of resilience, a life of dogged insistence. *She was on her own, nobody to stretch their hand and say, 'Here's a ten dollar, or a shilling,'* Carmen adds. *She was boasty too*, meaning she rejected any form of charity, insist-ing on her autonomy. How many times did she teeter on the edge of surrender? I wonder. How often did despair threaten to consume her? Nobody can say for sure, not even my mother. All she, Dwina, witnessed of Mama was an unyielding façade – a woman of steely resolve. Mama was not allowed to be vulnerable, and this must have been a source of pain.

If the soundscape of my childhood is defined by silence, it must also be because of the muteness produced by accumulated hurt. There's not a lot of dialogue in the memories

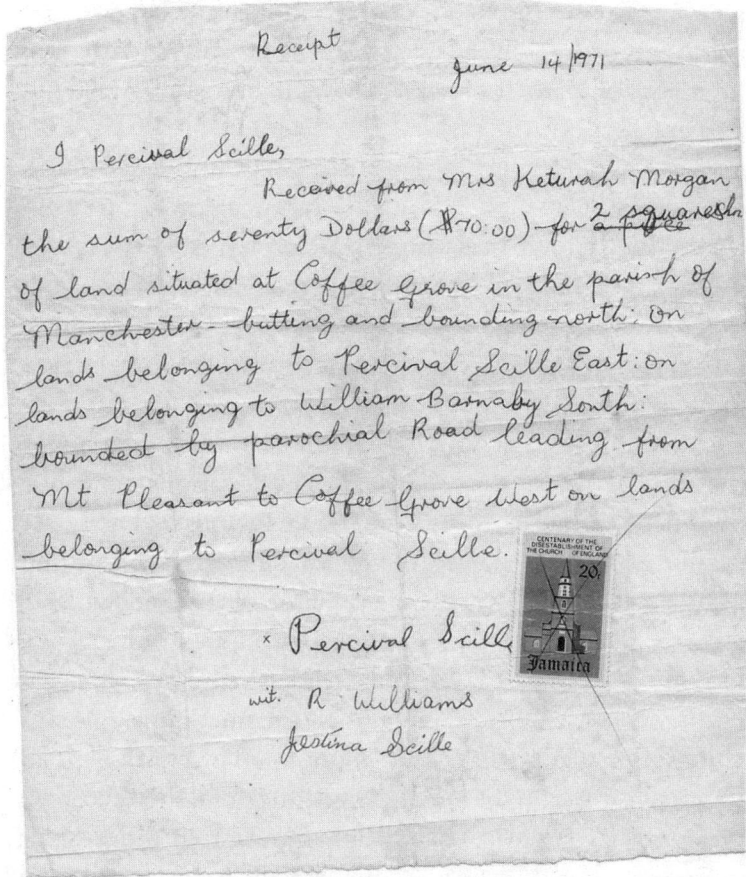

Deed of sale for '2 squares of land situated at Coffee Grove', which Mama purchased in 1971.

I have of my childhood. No conversations at the dinner table, no teasing between siblings, no squabbles between parents, no banter between a parent and their siblings who've come to visit. The very notion of family coming to visit was foreign to the world I knew. Come to think of it, there wasn't much discourse in my life, either, in the period after I moved with my mother. It's hard for me to conjure up snippets of teasing, of kidding around, of throwaway dialogue with her. There is a particular reason for this – the moments of levity that create dialogue, the kind of dialogue that one imagines in a novel or in the atmospheric parts of a film, were rare, if not absent. But isn't the reason for this absence (at least a part of it) the fact that my mother was also alone? Alone in a more brutal way than my grandmother. My mother had difficult relationships with men, much like Mama before her; she raised both her children – me and my sister, Charlene, born twelve years after me – alone. This aloneness of women is something that runs through the generations of my family, going back to the nineteenth century, to the decades after slavery. To a period in our family about which only scattered bits of information have been passed down. According to my mother, Mama's mother (my great-grandmother) and her baby-father's sister once shared the same man – wittingly or unwittingly, I do not know; this lasted for a while. This great-grandmother, Auntie Buss by name, had around eight children, some dying within months after birth. So many different fathers, but the fathers' names are not written on the birth certificates of the children.

Perhaps the difficulty of making up a family tree, any kind that would do justice to the concept of *family tree*, lies also in that fact. I look for the men of my family, and for their names in my memory, and find but few. Stories of the women abound; the men have been scattered. They are absent. Some are, no doubt, the husbands of other women, women who run stable families, families that are 'nuclear',

Portrait of my great-grandmother, Florence Neale, aka Auntie Buss (b.1887), with her niece and granddaughter. Taken at a studio in St Elizabeth in 1973.

the stain of the outside children ignored, unacknowledged. The children were *illegitimate. I* was illegitimate. The women in my family have illegitimate children, like me – they have always had. Except Mama, in her marriage with that man *who had a fault.*

Studio portrait of my great-great-grandmother, Margaret Ricketts (1867–1951). Date of photo unknown.

Shame is a silent emotion. The sound of shame *is* silence. Shame stills the fluency of speech and of laughter. Yet Mama protected me. Only now do I understand the silence. I had always known that my silence was more complex than bucolic. It was not the silence of the heath and the moors, which I discovered in the novels of Thomas Hardy; there was always something more complex below its surface. I was protected, yet my protection came at some cost I didn't know about, that I didn't *have* to know about, because by the time I came around, my grandmother had resolved to make the most of being alone. I'm grateful for my silent, green childhood, protected by both Mama and the bush.

I want to know who were the first Black settlers here, the first Black people to purchase land in Coffee Grove, you know, after slavery and all that, I mention to Miss Carmen.

Mommy jumps in. *Yes. I was just telling him what you told me. Ah nuh you father did own the land from here-so go right back to Mammy?* The spread of territory Mommy references includes the bit that was Mama's, now hers.

Carmen nods, confirming. *Stanley Williams, my grandfather, a him sell Mother Scille* [Mama's neighbour] *and her husband the land. Him own whole heap of land up here so.*

His original name was Bowells, Miss Carmen explains, *but him did have some mix-up in Ellen Street, where he was from, and run-weh come to Coffee Grove and buy up a lot of land.*

As Carmen unveils the story of her grandfather's journey, I'm left wondering: how did a man facing troubles elsewhere manage to reinvent himself and amass such wealth in a new district?

Ellen Street, but no de-so mi daddy come from?! Mommy exclaims, her eyes wide with excitement. *That's my father's natal district.* Her knowledge of his background is sketchy at best – presumably not because it's a secret, but rather because such matters were rarely discussed in those days. Once again, I face the muteness, a learned and practised silence, particularly of the emotional world, that gets locked behind a seldom if ever opened door. Again, this has everything to do with our history. It was easy to speak about work and toil, about the practical matters of eating and staying alive, but not about feelings, heritage and kinship.

I can't help but wonder whether this muteness has to do with how Daddy Joe, Mama and my other ancestors viewed their relationship with their space, with the way they conceived of their bodies within the spaces they occupied – as mere sojourners, people being kept alive, people living by default? Rather than, say, individuals who had a rightful claim to their space, who deserved to leave their imprint upon it, who had a right to their own inner world. And yet, as I've mentioned, I sense that my people have led such a rich life of the imagination – it must have been their source of resilience amid the horrors, hardships and dehumanisation they faced during slavery and its aftermath. But it wasn't very easy for them to place that inner life of the imagination into words: it seems words are always what fail under the effect of trauma. The least one can say is that both trauma and resilience have left their mark on my family.

Daddy Joe's ancestors, it appears, belonged to the Ellen Street clans who settled in the hillsides between Coffee Grove and Mount Pleasant. They were part of the peasantry supporting estates like the Whitney Plantation, which thrived in this area of north Manchester and Clarendon until the early twentieth century. Many of these estates have been unnamed to us until now, raising questions about the countless others we've never heard of – plantations cultivating coffee, hidden from our school textbooks. History, close yet obscure. There's so much that I hope to find in the archives, but gleaning a people's history of the land is equally vital. The journey begins here and now, I reassure myself, even if it entails long hours of walking, asking, looking and asking again – many trips from England; painstakingly slow but steady work.

Already, my mother and I are peering at Ellen Street through a new lens. Miss Carmen and my mother speculate that these individuals – my mother's paternal grandmother, known only by her nickname Ma Minky, along with Carmen's grandfather and others – likely arrived here in the late 1800s. Carmen begins to narrate, explaining that many residents of Ellen Street in south Manchester migrated to Coffee Grove, seeking employment at the Whitney Estate, a significant sugar and coffee plantation that still thrived in the latter part of the nineteenth century. My mother seems surprised by this revelation. Carmen paints a picture of hardship, food scarcity and a struggle for economic survival during that era. Ellen Street, it seems, was just one of the places from which people journeyed to this small community, which now stands as the centrepiece of my destiny.

While there's a deeper narrative waiting to be unearthed, filled with intricate details that remain beyond our reach, the question 'From where did we land here?' is beginning to get some answers, and I can take some comfort in that. Amidst this enquiry lies a narrative thread concerning Mama – a story we can sense but cannot fully access due to the many gaps and omissions in our family history, prompting us to fill in the blanks with our own imaginations.

Then there's the narrative thread concerning my grandfather, a topic I touch upon less here but one that warrants exploration in another tome. Coffee Grove houses my history because of him, too, and because of this curious history of migration that contains some fascinating stories of land, food and sustenance, and History with a big 'H'. There are a lot of stories buried in this history that beckon to be excavated. And from skeletal facts, the women – Miss Elaine, Miss Carmen and my mother – start to tell pure story, shooting the narrative ball from one person to the next, like a ping-pong match in words.

My mother's taken a picture of an old Polaroid photo and she's shared it with me via WhatsApp. In the photo, there is that fluffy white blooming, but of what is it the flower? I can't remember its name, and neither can Mommy. Its leaves are green all year, then turn to fluffy whiteness in December. In Coffee Grove, this was a sign of the approach of Christmas, with its cool breeze, the end of the year.

There are five men in the photo, and there's that flower, in bloom, behind them. First, there's Brother Gentles. His face is a friendly gruffness. Those eyebrows bushed with grey hairs and the eyes tucked under fat-rimmed folds and a broad forehead. He could smile, and could you know that he was smiling? Smiling was too much: how can you ask a man like this to smile? He knows how to make a woman pregnant. His sperm is functioning, and for him, Christ's way is to implant it. He has many children. Many dead wives, but many children. He wears a short tie, the tip of which is above the navel. It could be more accurately described as a symbol of the concept 'tie'. Who knows how to tie a tie when your work is grung and your impregnating is the work of Christ? Look at Brother G's green polka-dot tie, so fat, so stodgy, so unstylishly fat and stodgy and short.

They are all short, these ties.

Brother Hanson's is even lumpier, and shorter. So short it is almost not there.

And his face? Brother Hanson's face? It is the understudy of Pastor Wilson's. His face is Understudy. Faithful Follower. Called from sin and thankful to be accepted into the club.

Pastor Wilson's. His is slimmer, but still short, still above the navel. Who taught whom to tie their ties? Did they teach each other? No television then. No internet either, no smartphones with WhatsApp and videos shared by their children. Pastor Wilson the reader, the teacher, the carrier of a Bic pen stuck on the lapel of his jacket, cap twisted, because his last boy has played with it.

Brother Spencer with the beady eye. Is it glass? It is like days-old cabbage water with a thick, mucilaginous cap, translucent enough for you to see the pupil darting about underneath.

And Brother Goodison, the Sunday-school teacher, also impregnating in the name of Jesus.

All these are part of the road.

4.

The Teachings of Plants

Now and then, I find myself doing a double-take, almost incredulous that I'm actually here, sleeping and waking in my native hillside district. As I sit on my veranda, breathing in the morning dew, a cup of mint tea in hand, I retrieve the lost familiarity of a cutlass sliding over grass, clinking on rocks, as a farmer leads her goats to pasture, her water boots thudding on stones. Images come to me now of Mama walking through the woodlands, going to common to 'tie out goat' or to grung, her cultivation plot.

It's early morning and the dew is still on the grass. First, we walk along beaten footpaths, then gradually move through rough grassland as Mama clears a way through tall bushes with a stick. She's looking for three specific herbs ('bushes', we call them). She does not remember the names of all three. They were 'given' to her in a dream; she needs to make a tea with them to cure her cough, which is now developing into bronchitis. She remembers the names, and the very character, of two (sarsaparilla, John Charles; she's deeply acquainted with these plants), but if she's walking and looking like this – slowly, moving the grass with her stick, craning her neck, bending – it's because scanning the bush will help her recall what the third one was. Bushes and plants have power, and we depend on them; this is self-evident, a knowledge carried in our bodies – a kind of archive passed down from generation to generation – so this way of walking and looking practised by the grown-ups here, not just Mama, conveys a deep awareness of the powers the plants have.

I consider now the way she walked, which had everything to do with the way she looked at the land that surrounded her. She would walk with one arm gripping the other behind her back, the way Jamaican 'country people' do while examining the bush. It was an engaged way of looking around; it had so much familiarity in it, but what it had most was a sort of expectation. I have probably never thought about this before now and it must have always seemed normal to me, this way of hers, which was the way of many people in the district. Mammy Scille, the old woman whose property abutted our own, also walked in the same manner. In my mind's eye, I see this body language in everyone who ever walked in a bush in Coffee Grove.

In Mama's dream, it was always three or five herbs, odd numbers; according to tradition, the number should never be even. I've never heard the reason behind this, nor do I know anyone who has; it has always been *just so*, and the belief has exerted a fascination on my imagination, a curiosity for practices from whose sources we have been disconnected.

One of us might have been ill and the dream revealed the precise concoction she needed to make to cure us. As she looked around while walking, she may have been scanning the bush to remember the particular ones she'd been given in the dream, or to remember which one or ones she'd forgotten. One could never be sure, as she would never reveal the precise contents of her dream until she had performed the acts that it solicited. This is also tradition.

We used many bushes in our home back then. As a child,

I grew to know their uses. Fever grass was evidently for fever, and only when I moved to England did I learn that it was, in fact, called 'lemon grass' by the English and other people, who also use it for its healing properties. I still find magic, however, in our naming of herbs based on their therapeutic or medicinal uses, as it seems to reveal something about our thinking and our history. Naming is storytelling, and that form of naming betokens its own particular relationship to the plant. From a certain point of view, that relationship may seem reductive in its emphasis on the plant's utility, but in another sense, it's a relationship of proximity and intimacy, one that conveys a sense of vulnerability, for knowing this grass as *fever grass* is also an expression of dependence. Here, particularly in the countryside, people care very little about English or European botanical names or Latin classifications. As if to highlight that fact, and to subvert the European names, Jamaicans have also conferred English names on local plants that may be radically different in identity. For us, dandelion is an aromatic shrub that grows seeds in a long, slender pod. The only thing suggestive of the dandelions that constellate every springtime in Roundhay Park is the yellowness of their small flowers; not even the shape is the same. Sage, marigold and plantain, among others, have had similar fortunes.

As a child, I imagined that jointa was associated with the joints of the body and used for associated complaints. In my mind, the name followed the same logic as fever grass and search mi heart, herbs named after the condition or part of the body they're particularly good at treating. Search mi heart conveyed more mystery than jointa, however, as I grew up in the devoutly religious environment of the village with its Church of God, in which Anglo-Saxon Protestantism blended with African gestural repertoires and music. The African element constantly sought to free itself and express a spirituality of its own, but was always restrained, tempered, by a corporeality that was different from it, more 'respectable'. Growing up in strict religious environments is the reality of a great many Jamaicans of country and of town, but the closed atmosphere of the hamlet, which seemed unaware of any other people except its own, intensified this devoutness. The community had only itself as reference, since in those days people seldom travelled outside the district. Things were slightly looser for people who had the privilege of going to school – my mother was one of those. It was precisely *because* of her schooling that I spent my early years with my grandmother. She was at teachers' college, and had me somewhere in the middle, I reckon, of her time there. She was twenty-one years old when I was born, a naïve young girl who must have never had a boyfriend until she fell upon my father, whom I have only very recently met.

Growing up with my grandmother, I perceived herbal medicine to be a natural part of our everyday life. To say *perceived* may be inaccurate, since one never thought about such things, one simply lived them; we lived with plants – with our bushes. I've lost the names of many of them now, but a few of the intriguing ones return, which also happen to be some of the ones my mother, Dwina, gives to me, packed in Ziploc bags, each time I'm returning to England from a trip home. Search mi heart made me think not only of the physical heart – I imagined the properties of the weed moving through and inspecting the cardiac ventricles while the individual slept – but also of that spiritual inner place, the elusive one, which we refer to as 'the heart', and I wondered, then, why people should want to associate the idea of spiritual cleansing with a plant.

Already, I was fascinated by the names left behind for things; they were relics and remnants of an event or of a particular revelation – the residues of the stories that are within them. Take the bush called John Charles, for instance. Who was he, and what led to a plant being named after him? Other bushes follow the logic of medicinal or pharmacopoeial usage, sometimes comically. Consider, for example, inflation weed. Knowing the bawdy humour of our ancestors, I assume now that this weed may refer, mockingly, to the problem of impotence that it is meant to treat. Other bush names are less 'indicative', but have no less a sense of vernacular poetry: leaf of life, guinea-hen weed, strong back, sarsaparilla, chainy root, Jack ina bush.

But this issue of the names of bushes and of the intimacies they convey relates very much to my peasant people's way of walking. It strikes me that knowing the bush like this means that one is not a passive walker. For Mama, Mammy Scille and so many farmers and dwellers in Coffee Grove, knowledge of trees and plants was not just scientific. What was significant about trees and bushes was not merely the rationality of why we need them; the need to engage with them was equally, if not more, important, and I saw that engagement every day, in so many forms. There was a kind of respect shown towards the woodlands.

It's day four of my trip to Jamaica. After walking for more than an hour, I'm tired. I sit on the sharp grooves of a limestone rock; my backside is uncomfortable. I'm happy to enjoy a bit of rest while Congolin, the herbalist Rasta I've befriended, goes off to help his farmer brethren retrieve a thousand-dollar note lost somewhere on this hillside. I met Congolin yesterday in the street, right here in Coffee Grove. *A dis a di man yu need fi talk to!* Mama's old friend Maas Lisha had declared, his eyes beaming as he used his head to point to Congolin, a short, skinny Rastaman with friendly eyes and a permanently affixed smile.

When I meet him, he is wearing a small backpack, which I imagine might contain herbs. I stand at the roadside, listening to him speak to the group of men gathered there. The men listened attentively and with respect to the authoritative medicine man. Knowledge poured out of him about all sorts of plants, ones I had known and others about which I had no clue; plants whose uses I'd heard about and others whose virtues I'd never suspected; the things he's managed to do that have baffled even the doctors.

Knowing that I was coming today, he's prepared an entire pile of bushes for me to take back to England. He's laid these out on a crocus bag, which he has placed on a rock outside the door to the hut located at the bottom of his farm. This is not where he sleeps. He lives in the village, but prepares his meals on a wood fire in the hut and takes his daily naps there. *Take your medicine with you,* he says, *I know your granny must did boil nuff a these when you a pickney.* He picks them up one by one to tell me their names and usages, though I know some of them already. But all of these – all twenty-one of them – can be boiled together to make a potent mixture. *Anyway,* he adds, *when you crush up all a dem-ya together, you won't even know which is which, but you will know se it's all there and you will smell and taste the different ones-dem.*

Nerve wiss, which removes toxins from the blood, calms

the nerves and cleans the liver. Cow-foot leaf, the muscle relaxant, relieves back pain. Mary Goules is healing when used for growths, skin ulcers and sores. It will also benefit me as a cleanser for the bloodstream. Dandelion is for strengthening the heart. John Charles is great for treating asthma. Boil nedge weed with peanut trash and medina, he instructs me, for a powerful nerve tonic. Wild plantain (the bush they call plantain in England) heals wounds and sores when used in baths, and cures kidney problems. Velvet, almost as bitter as cerasee, is beneficial for *hammering colds*, he tells me, *for pounding dem out of the body.* So is running crocus, which, when you boil it, *is almost as red as your blood.* Likewise, trumpet and cup and saucer are good *cold bushes*, and excellent for maintaining a strong immune system. Tan pon rock, otherwise known as consumption weed, is another immune-system booster and, according to Congolin, increases the desire for frequent sex in both women and men. And there are sticks and roots: yellow stick, ramoon and breadnut bark. A lot of these roots and herbs don't grow in backyard gardens, since they like the cool darkness of woodlands. Congolin is the type of person who will go looking for them in their habitat, trekking over hills to find the right ones. That's what you do when you're a country medicine man. That's what he did to gather a number of the bushes, wisses and roots that are in this pile, and I'm humbled.

But above all, what strikes me is the *way* he talks about plants – with love, as if they were darlings. *Eternal Father, Divine Mother, please give me the blessing and the gift to hear from the plants* . . . is a prayer he formulates every morning. *The woman have a big role to play, you can't leave har outta di concept,* he clarifies: for him, God is both male and female. He speaks of the plants whispering to him, and I'm curious about what this feels like. He describes it as experiencing the plants' joy, entering into a sort of empathy with them in which he can comprehend their emotions. *Plants have feelings*, he insists, *you have to understand them if you goin use them. You can't just use them based on your selfish longing, you haffi really love the plants them if you want them fi work. The plants them don't give the same power every day and the same time every day.*

Being a herbalist involves acknowledging the communicative nature of plants. While I've instinctively felt this since I was a child growing up with Mama, it's something I was never taught in my biology classes in high school. In fact, it seems to go against those lessons. Some might denounce this sort of thinking as anti-science, but this is the basis of Congolin's practice, and of an entire relationship to plants – for him, but also for all those in the community who turn to him because of their beliefs. Is it possible to entertain the idea that plants also seek to communicate with us? This might mean entertaining the notion that Western science is not the *only* science that exists.

I'm from a community of people who believe that things can speak, and that our people have the ability to hear and understand their speech. It's this perspective that piques my curiosity about Congolin's insights. The scholar part of me wants to probe: *What does the whisper sound like? How exactly do the plants whisper to you?* The answer he provides offers no greater clarity than his previous statement – *You have a complaint or a sickness within you, and I ask the Father for the knowledge, to open my blind eyes.* We've gone into the realm of the visual now, despite his assertion that the plants communicate with him through whispers. But perhaps his answers can't be 'clarifying' in the way I expect. As a poet, you know that sense perceptions are often fluid and untranslatable, and you often grope for the best image you can find to translate for your readers what you feel. It's often about approximations, because, after all, we may occasionally see sound. We may even taste it. It's probably just impossible to translate dream language, just like, for a poet, it's impossible to convey what you really feel, hear and see; the attempt is made nevertheless. Certain things may not become clear today, if at all.

I always give thanks to Father, he continues, saying:

> *'Give thanks for your great concept of healing.' This a something me pray for you know, me ask Father fi bless me with great healing concep' of herbs fi heal the sickness in me. Then one of the time me get a vision, a me Auntie me vision see, and she show me one bush – me have a certain sickness – and say fi use this bush, and if it good fi me, it good fi others. And me use up the bush, rub it pon me; anywhere me a feel pain, the pain diminish.*

Many stories of healing involve an episode such as this, in which a dead loved one *dreams* the sick person and reveals to them what herbs they need to use and how. This dream might be the result of 'prayer'. But it does seem that prayer may be broadly understood here, not necessarily as a request to the Christian God, but as a request to the ancestors and to the plants themselves. *A nuh muss wud yuh a talk outta yuh mout, enuh*: Congolin reaches out to the plants themselves through the intensity of his yearning – plant telegraphy. For people like him who live and see between worlds, it's this attentiveness and this yearning, more powerful and precise than words, that are reciprocated in the form of a dream: *a night time, when yuh a sleep, is like yuh soul rise up outta yuh body fi go meet wid di plant-dem.* You could say that the plant dream is something that happens when the desires of the plant meet the desires of the person seeking its power. Favouring these encounters involves practising certain attitudes, cultivating certain dispositions, he explains to me, but he is reticent to go into further details. Overall, Congolin's descriptions reflect an epistemology inherent to my upbringing – the fact that plants *also* have desire. His practice is based on a system, which might be closer to Jamaican *siyans* than to Western science. He certainly has developed a method for his work. This science has meaning; it also has a history, if an unwritten one.

Meanwhile, along the roadside, as we descend the hill, we see clumps of wild sage and, underneath them, leaf of life. He takes pleasure in naming the bushes. I am realising both how many I already know and how many there are to discover. It seems we could spend the entire afternoon on the road like this, because almost every bush has an identity, even if it has no name that can be found in a book. Now, he points to the Jack ina bush, recounting how he's used it to treat prostate cancer. Now he points to donkey weed, and I'm too busy recording the information about its uses to even take a photo of the herb. Would I be able to identify it, if I saw it in a week, tomorrow? So many unwritten stories. *All this a medicine you know, it powerful so till* – gesturing towards a pomegranate tree. When he points out *memory weed* to me, I realise that it's the same herb I've encountered in England as *rosemary*.

It's a pleasure to share like this, and for each bush, there are multiple stories of healings – within one's family, of an individual one knows, of someone one hears about, of a legend – and dreams. Always the dreams. Dreams, healing and herbs: they work together.

*

In Jamaica, there's a particular kind of dream that people call a 'vision'. Some, like Congolin, differentiate 'vision' from 'dream'. According to him, a vision is when *something come clear to you – a same so you see it, a so it go* ; whereas a dream *don't walk straight, you haffi interpret it. Vision a the thing that you see and it come tru quick.* It's in the morning when he's about to wake up that visions generally come to him. He describes himself at these moments as being in a liminal state, neither quite awake nor quite asleep, conscious of everything happening around him. In fact, it's as if he's out of his body, looking down at himself. *That is when the plants come to talk to me.* The plants make him 'hear' their voice by showing him images of which ones he's to *pick*, in what combinations, and images of the people (friends, family) they're for. He's not in this as a business. Living a modest life in a small home he shares with his sister, he travels miles on foot, embracing a simple lifestyle. If the people he helps find it in their conscience to offer him some money as a thank you, then he's grateful. For him, this gift of visions and the *great knowledge of whispering sound* are things to be shared rather than sold. *Them say me mad,* he continues, *but I say a great intelligence of madness.*

Congolin's own plot of land is an astonishment. To call it farmland is almost to mischaracterise it. It cotches on the flank of an extremely craggy karst limestone hill, projecting rocks that stand erect in the earth like megaliths. Upon closer inspection, however, they appear as what they truly are: undersea rocks. I see the holes, notice the pathways that water has created, holes running to where one cannot see, sharp crevices and runnels in the white rock that gleams under the sun, dazzling the eyes. There are lots of them, everywhere, and the slope is extremely steep.

Climbing up and through Congolin's cultivations, and periodically looking behind me at the steep drop below, I'm amazed at what he has done here. For many, this land would be considered uncultivable. I'm watching my step, anxious about pitching over the hillside all the way down into the wild tangle of lianas and untouched trees that conceal, per-haps, some chasm below me. I'm also trying to avoid stepping on the carrot shoots planted everywhere. Congolin walks with assured steps up and across the hillside, on land that to me seems precarious, even dangerous. Where I want to watch my step, move gingerly, to avoid pitching back-wards and onto the pointed rocks beneath, he seems to eat up the hillside, taking no visible care about where and how he positions his feet. The tiny spaces between the rocks brim with cultivation. There is yellow and negro yam, banana, plantain, papaya, okra, sugar beans and all sorts of trees – avocado, pimento, castor, guinep and more – on this flank of the hill. I'd not have been able to imagine so many things growing here because of the sheer smallness – what to *me* is smallness – of the cultivable space. But Congolin forces me to see this space differently, to adopt a radically different vision of scale. For Congolin, this land is not forbidding; it's what is available to him and what it's his privilege to work with, to live with.

But Congolin also plants yams: barby, white afu, yellow afu. In the Akan language, the word *Afúw* means 'farm', which should say a lot about the significance of the yam. Afu is just one of the many Akan words that we have in Jam-iekan, aka Patwa. *Some yam haffi plant under the sign of the new moon*, Congolin mentions at one point, instantly evoking

Mama and her almanac – 'under the sign of the new moon' means a few days after the full moon. For instance, it is necessary to plant the yellow afu three days after the moon is full. Our people know that if you don't wait until three days after the full moon to plant the yellow afu, it will grow, but it won't grow straight; it will grow bulging and round into what our people call pum-pum yam. The pum-pum yam tastes just as good but holds less value, less allure in the marketplace. There's an underlying gendered undertone to this perception: the straight yam, undoubtedly a phallic symbol, reigns as the ultimate prize. Other yams, like mozella, Sinvinsen, barby and taw, can be planted on the day of the new moon.

Clambering over stones, we eventually get to Congolin's 'hills' of yellow afu. He planted them in August and plans to reap them in August of next year. After a year in the ground, the yellow afu is 'very ripe'. Cooked at this point, it is pleasingly soft. Beyond a year in the ground – some people do leave it there that long – it becomes 'clammy'. *It's dangerous dem time-de*, he says, as it now has copious amounts of starch, which equals lots of sugar in the bloodstream. Which is why, in health terms, it's better to harvest the yellow afu at around the nine-month mark.

The sociologist and writer Erna Brodber has declared that yam symbolises the links between Africa and its diaspora, noting that the breaking of yams among the Akan in Ghana at the beginning of the year is a symbolic act of sharing the basics of life. For Brodber, visiting Ghana and observing yam in Akan traditional life offered insights into its significance within Jamaican peasant culture. These traditions, carried over by our Akan ancestors, continue to shape who we are today. The breaking of the yams, which marks the start of the Akan year, highlights our own linguistic connections. As Brodber points out, yam is so integral to life among this people that the words for 'food' and for 'eat' resemble the word *yam*. The word *ninyam* (food), which we have in our Patwa, exemplifies this connection. Cassidy and Le Page, in their *Dictionary of Jamaican English*, also note this link, which they say goes back to a number of West African and Bantu languages brought to Jamaica.

'Back in Woodside [the name of Brodber's district, itself a former coffee plantation], I had the fascinating experience of digging a yam hill,' she wrote to me in an email; 'it is so like taking a baby.' This anecdote seemed to encapsulate the deep intimacy I perceived between people and yam in our culture.

In her essay 'Novel and History, Plot and Plantation', the Jamaican critic and philosopher Sylvia Wynter tells us that it was 'around the growing of yam, of food for survival' that African peasants transplanted to the plot (the measly bits of land they were given to cultivate on the slavery estates) created a folk culture. For these Africans, she writes, 'the land remained the earth'. They used it to feed themselves, 'and to offer first fruits to the earth'.

But the fact that yam growing requires inherited knowledge and commitment also explains why some of them have almost disappeared from the scene today: there just aren't enough people around to learn and practise the skills needed to produce negro yam, for instance, a variety requiring much technical knowledge and care.

All right, look ya. Congolin directs me to look at some beans near one of his yam patches. They look diminished. *Why you believe insect cut them down? . . . Because it plant under wrong sign . . . Me was to plant it close to the dark night* [when the moon is about to be new again]; *that way, no insect would damage it.* And in other terms, here's what he's saying: insects – like crickets – are out there to 'fight against' the plant. If he'd planted the beans on the dark night, the crickets wouldn't be able to 'attack' it as much: *scientific powers of planting*, remarks Congolin, with a cackle.

Whether it's beans or yams, the young people aren't as interested in the traditional methods:

The young people them say our planting method a olden days. Now a technology days, them say. But some of these 'new technologies' not so good fi wi . . . Even the yam stick out of fashion now. You have man planting yam now and covering it with tarpaulin, nothing for the vine fi run pon. Height o' madness! Them yam-de full a water and tasteless. The amount of knowledge what require, it nuh simple, so that quick thing that some of the young people a-do, them can't touch down inna di right order.

Tell me something, I say, as we walk back down the hill. *How come you decide fi plant grung up yasso, pon di hillside?* I can't help but ask.

Well, no only it me have? he says to me; he's perhaps anticipated the question, which he has no doubt been asked before. But he looks at me instructively, calmly, as if to say, *a dat you haffi know* – you need to understand this. Around Jamaica, there must be loads of cultivation grungs like this, on precarious hillsides, perched on rocky flanks, as if they could fall off, as if the farms could roll down the mountains, but their farmers cultivate them anyway. To engineer space is part of who we are as a people. As we've made life in this land, cultivating an aesthetic out of the impossible is a necessity we have come to know over the centuries, not just an innate instinct. Is there

75

a kind of thrill in the capacity to do this? A part of the thrill may be the security Congolin gets from the tenure of this land, deemed unwanted, the security of knowing he won't be challenged for this space. This is rejected land – there are links with our history here. Finding the physical space in which you can be free, a space that can be yours, as an African living on this island, which for so long was under the control of colonists, often meant appropriating impracticable, forbidding pieces of land, the land considered undesirable to the colonists themselves, or which they couldn't access.

Congolin's demeanour changes when he's in this space; it's his, he owns it. This is a feeling I'd like to be able to experience in Leeds, but how does one even begin to own that feeling there, when so little land is actually wild or cultivated self-sustainably like this, and when so little of that cultivable land can belong to ordinary folk? The only option I see is an allotment, which a few of my friends have. They get a certain sense of fulfilment from being able to grow some food; some even see city allotments, those tiny patches of earth, as a resistance to industrialised food chains, and they're right of course; I get that. Sometimes I think, *heck, I should be getting an allotment too*, but could the allotment ever compare to the joy of embracing and stewarding an area of grung like this? That said, in Leeds, through my networks of friends, I've started to seek out food-growing associations and support groups for people who want to grow and work towards food independence. I seek out such groups and follow them on social media. My wife, Lucile, and I have started to talk about what we could do with the space available to us, i.e. the balcony of our flat. For now, we've planted some bulbs of garlic, and recently I've started to notice some sprouts forming in the little pots we've filled with soil purchased from Tesco. We've planted some rosemary, some basil and some cherry tomatoes. It's a start.

Looking at Congolin's space, and what he's made of it, brings to mind Esiah Levy, a Black train driver turned farmer in the UK. Levy's relationship to the soil was one that astonished many in the years before his untimely death in 2019, and has been the object of newspaper and magazine articles. He came to the attention of many because of his attempts to encourage food growing amongst the young population in Britain, particularly among the demographics that have been most alienated from the land – which includes, of course, Black Britons, a number of whose ancestors hail from the West Indies. Levy's parents were themselves Jamaican.

But one of the main things that made this story of seeds and planting interesting is that Levy lived in the big city, London, and cultivated his crops on a very limited parcel of land, 'barely 15 by 9 feet', as Ruby Tandoh notes in her article 'Empire of Seeds'. Her remark that Levy's tiny farm was 'packed with an astonishing 23 trees' sends my mind directly back to Congolin's land, in which Levy's determination to make the most of his acreage finds a striking parallel. Levy was showing just how much could be done with a tiny backyard plot, just how much food could be grown – how much people could feed themselves in a self-sufficient manner, reducing their dependence on globalised food chains, in a country like England – and that idea proved attractive to many. Numerous people who felt alienated from the earth, from the foods they consume, and who asked questions about globalised neoliberal economics and its effects on food, found in Levy's work something that was new and deeply inspiring. I can't help but think that what Levy was doing in 2017 and 2018 resembles what Congolin is practising silently on this hillside, far away from the cameras of the British media.

At high school in Jamaica, I received an education about what poverty was, and Coffee Grove was an example of it – even as my mother flailed in the waters of IMF economics under Jamaica's neoliberal government of the 1990s, when the term 'structural adjustment' was a part of our daily soundscape, constantly in the news. Structural adjustment was something bad, I knew, but it took me a while – I needed more experience of the world – to understand that this term referred to the fiscal policies that the IMF imposed on governments in exchange for their loans.

By this time, I had left Coffee Grove and was living in Porus with my mother. If we didn't understand the theory behind structural adjustment, we understood all too well what it meant for us – falling or frozen wages, an inexorable decline in standards of living, the devaluation of the Jamaican dollar, rampant inflation, lots of Idaho potatoes, American corn, American apples, American foods of all kinds on the supermarket shelves. All the produce that our farmers cultivated in abundance was now being replaced by American substitutes. And all of a sudden, the American ones were cheaper. There was an all-of-a-suddenness to the 1990s for my mother, as for many other people. Yet here we were in Porus, having left the rural behind. And that's why we never stopped to think about 'nature'. On the one hand, we were trying to escape the rural lifestyle of hands in the grung; on the other, we couldn't afford the trappings of a middle-class lifestyle. We went to the beach once a year, for instance – a grand outing on a big coach, a once-yearly opening of the windows onto this 'bigger life' of which my mother had dreamed.

A season of wonders is how I'd describe this trip to Jamaica. I marvel at the variety of colours in the beans that come out of the sugar bean pods – all of which are from the same root – on Congolin's plot. Marvel at the abundance of carrots he gives me and from which I wash away the dirt; marvel at my own hands in the dirt, at seeing things grow, at seeing ginger rhizomes with their stalks, the thyme that covers Congolin's farm. I marvel at how many things can come from a small plot of land. Being able to touch the source of the food I eat is exhilarating. I even marvel at the twine that Congolin uses to tie my thyme and scallions together – giant bulbs of scallions, humongous bunches of thyme. The sight of the twine leads me to fantasise about an economy without plastic. I can see what a plastic-free economy used to look like. I witness remnants of a plastic-free imaginary.

During my time in Jamaica, my meals consist predominantly of locally sourced ingredients from Coffee Grove. As I arrange my provisions on the kitchen counter, I am struck by the vibrant array before me. Okra fills one bowl, while another holds an assortment of ground provisions – yams, sweet potatoes, green bananas and plantains – essential fuel for my treks through the hills. Scallions, thyme and garlic are scattered in random piles, freshly harvested from Congolin's farm. May-May's ginger adds a spicy kick, complementing the ripe bananas, soursop, sweetsop and avocados. A cardboard box houses sweet cassava flour, spices, condiments and a bottle of honey procured from a roadside stall near Porus.

This abundance of food exceeds my personal needs, prompting me to share it with my mother during visits or to offer the extra to my neighbour downstairs. The provisions here contrast starkly with the contents of my cupboard back in Leeds, where my wife and I purchase the best available foods and where our weekly market trips yield Caribbean and African ground provisions and fresh fish. The scarcity and expense of natural foods in Leeds stand in sharp contrast to the abundance and affordability here in Coffee Grove.

In England, our culinary preferences reflect a blend of cultural influences shaped by my wife's French heritage and our children's upbringing in that country. Having lived in Europe for many years, my culinary habits have evolved to embrace richer, albeit less nutritious, fare. Despite my occasional indulgence in decadent treats, I remain mindful of their impact on my health, acknowledging the allure of foods that tantalise the taste buds but compromise well-being. I reminisce about those late nights as a grad student in Oxford, where the perfect finale to club or party escapades was a serving of deep-fried chips crowned with grated Cheddar and lavishly slathered in mayo and ketchup. Migration, I've learned, introduces you to a vast array of culinary adventures.

Yet, amidst the allure of exotic foods, I can't help but ponder the subtle influences shaping my dietary choices. Acculturation and notions of socio-cultural superiority often dictate our culinary preferences. Some foods and drink, like Coca-Cola or pizza, become symbols of Western cosmopolitanism, while others infiltrate non-Western societies through the pervasive reach of globalisation. Food consumption intersects with history and geopolitical power, just as migration does. The values I've assimilated – pun intended – around food, about what's good and what's desirable, around what's a good meal, also have to do with a history of colonialism. In Jamaica, globalisation has also meant that people consume far more processed foods than existed in the diets of their forebears. These older diets weren't necessarily healthy either. The regimens imposed on our enslaved forebears contained elements that contributed to diminished life expectancies. Significantly, however, dietary habits brought from Africa persisted, despite deportation and the losses it entrained. These are the habits I try to embrace.

But to go back to my kitchen counter in Coffee Grove: it has me thinking long and hard about food independence and how I've been disconnected from it; in fact, it's not just the mere fact of food independence that matters, it's how we've been disconnected from the ability to care for other living beings, our relations. For me, then, being excited about all this wholesome food that I get from Coffee Grove and from Congolin is not only about the urge to eat healthily, it's also about the excitement of reconnecting with ways of living with the land – the food is only a part of that.

After my first trip to Congolin's farm, I spend several days going back to see him, and it. I refer to the place as his 'plantation' and he grins his silent, mischievous grin. Today there's a cool breeze. It's hard to find a place to sit because the rocks are too craggy. I eventually find a spot and we keep conversing as he flits nimbly about, chattering endlessly, moving from one topic to the next:

Sugar cane to preserve roots tonic just made.
Rat and mongoose eating out yam head.
Slugs eating down my beans.
The vicissitudes of the farm life.

In this moment, it is not necessarily the things I have not seen before that strike me, rather the things I perceive with greater intensity or focus. I notice the fluttering of the banana leaves in the wind. The leaves are like pennons, their sound a gentle but constant chorus. I also notice that Congolin is alone. However, now, I find this kind of solitude remarkable, this sort of working by oneself, which obviously reminds me of Mama working her grung alone, though her aloneness was in many ways a difficult one, something she had to make her peace with. I myself have been known to like solitude, being alone among things that grow and change.

When I was a child, I enjoyed planting things. In fact, I planted cowpeas and they grew and gave quite healthy crops on several occasions. With each successful harvest, my fondness for the act of planting only deepened. There is something visceral about witnessing the seeds you've sown with your own hands transform into plants and then into food. Indeed, I find something physically gratifying about witnessing a banana sucker take root, find space, adapt to the earth in which it's planted and become its own plant. In a sense, the soil takes hold of it, as soil and shoot form something new in conjunction with each other. When that shoot becomes a new thing, I experience feelings of exultation at seeing different beings from the ones that existed the day before – especially when this transformation is witnessed in the early morning. And, in fact – such is the elation of a child – as I planted my beans (my cowpeas) and tried my hand at corn (in a soil that proved to be shallow, clayey and resistant) in the yard of the house my mother rented in Porus, my first thought upon waking in the morning would be to go out into the little front-yard garden to look at the new changes that had appeared.

The French word *jouissif* is what comes nearest to describing the feeling of witnessing this transformation, which is something close to, it seems to me now, the awakening to an erotic life. I say *witnessing*, being cognisant, of course, that one hasn't truly *witnessed*; one has merely arrived at the scene of something that has already taken place. The sorrow that comes about when you're faced with that sense of the impossible! Life's metamorphosis, both beneath and above the soil, unfolds incessantly, though its subtlety and gradual pace often escape our notice. Yet, in the morning light, these seemingly imperceptible changes appear as monumental leaps, astonishing transformations. Perhaps these changes are, in fact, rapid, and we simply aren't around to see them. Oh, all the exciting things that must happen on this peasant plantation at night!

For a while, I'm caught up in this memory of planting. Congolin has not stopped talking since I've arrived at his grung, and now what he's saying suddenly has my attention: *When the sun come up and a day time, the plants them a wuk haad* [they are working hard], *yu haffi leave them alone, in peace.* It is his way of explaining why one should gather plants just after sunrise but never after sunset, since, according to him, plants go to sleep at night. As simple as that. Said with disarming ingenuousness. As if to say that in their personhood, plants resemble us more than we might think. Do plants also dream – do they dream *us*? If plants really do sleep at nights, then it is perhaps when they sleep that they're at their most fanciful, prodigious, creative.

Am I beginning to understand the fascination that the magic of plants exerts on Congolin's imagination? It strikes me now that this magic is a quiet one, understated, that you can't see it until you *see it*. Meaning, until you live around it, with it, amongst it. This perhaps is the benefit – the joy – of solitude among the trees and plants. A kind of jealously guarded intimacy with the things, and the *jouissance* of seeing them grow. This is itself a form of dreaming. By dreaming, what I'm talking about is the possibility of being with the land in this way. For many people in England, the ability to have one's hands in the soil like this is a dream. It's the kind of magic that people in Britain have been cut off from. And immigrants more than any other group – it's hard for us to acquire the soil, the earth, the space in which to live this way.

It's impossible to talk about dreaming and the urge to dream – about having *time* to dream – without talking about capitalism and what it does to the bodies that are most vulnerable to it. In Britain and other northern countries, many of them former colonising nations, some of capitalism's most terrible violences reside in the bodies of Black folks. Black people are overrepresented among the overworked and exhausted, among those 'caught up in the hustle and shenanigans of white supremacy and capitalism', to use the words of the activist Tricia Hersey, author of the book *Rest is Resistance*. In such positions, it's difficult to have the time and space to dream – to *literally* dream, in the calm of sleep, but also to daydream, with all that that implies with respect to time and space. I have come to the conclusion, like Hersey, that connecting back to our dreams and to the dreamworld, *in the most literal sense* – dreams connect us to the living world in powerful ways – swaddles us back to our deepest selves. Dreaming is a portal to freedom, but I think, too, that being in connection with the land *helps* us to dream. Again, I mean *literally* dream, but *dream* could also be synonymous here with being in tune with those ways in which the earth communicates with us, with tapping into those empower-ing senses that have been numbed by capitalism, or, to quote the poet Jorie Graham, those 'earlier, more ancient, human feelings of belonging in creation'. Dreaming, then, not as opposition to being awake, but, actually, its intensification.

As happens so often while we're together, Congolin 'intro-duces' me to a new herb. Amidst casual conversation, he interjects with a knowing smile, *You know da one ya?* Or, *Me know se you know this one* – testing me. This time he merely says, *Smell this.* This bush is called *fresh cut.* I put it to my nos-trils and do not want to remove it. The herb smells like the formic acid secreted by ants – less sickly sweet, however; rather, deep and penetrating, like anise. Often, I consider smell, with its nuanced layers of sensation, the most forceful of the senses, yet the most difficult to capture in words.

Congolin has the map of his territory inscribed within him; he knows every rock and crevice of the land. Now that he's here, he exudes a kind of confidence one might call owner's confidence. Only those who have it can talk to themselves the way he does, grumbling about the dogs trampling his cabbages and his carrot sprouts, planning out loud what he's going to get from up top to *add to the pot* that's on fire.

In his book *Fugitive, Where Are You Running?*, Dénètem Touam Bona speaks of 'rehabilitating the power of dreams and poetry to ward off the confinement of minds and bodies'. For the Maroons, those Africans who fled the plantations and set up autonomous communities within the hinterlands of colonised territories across the Americas, dreams had real, operative power. Dreaming was part of their medicinal system, part of their relationship with the green world, as it was for my own grandmother. It represented an overall attitude to life and a form of resistance. The British settlers often feared the Maroons for their deep familiarity with the mountainous territories, which were beyond the control of the colonists. In Jamaica, for instance, the Maroons on the windward side of the island, under their leader Queen Nanny, waged a successful war against the British in the eighteenth century, which culminated in a peace treaty that recognised the right of Nanny, her people and their heirs to control a parcel of 500 acres in the parish of Portland. The Windward Maroons' extensive knowledge of the rugged terrain of the Blue and John Crow Mountains enabled them to manoeuvre stealthily and conduct raids on plantations, causing substantial economic damage. Their understanding of the environment, enriched by ancestral wisdom and insights into Caribbean ecology, further strengthened their resistance efforts. The historian Werner Zips underscores the importance of an 'elaborate ecological knowledge' in conjunction with their military tactics in his book *Nanny's Asafo Warriors*.

The *dream attitude* is characterised by the ingenuity of those whose physical freedom was restricted, yet who creatively found within their bodies the resources that kept their imaginations and worlds alive. Dreams and the green world were key to this, and to the Maroons' concept of healing in a seventeenth- and eighteenth-century context, where access to medical doctors was unimaginable. Marronage was not just a physical fugue. Certainly it was that, but it was perhaps just as importantly a fugue of imagination and of creativity. In practising their kind of intimacy with plants and with the dream world, people who have endured their – our – history of subjugation can experience the emergence of what French historian Sylvie Chalaye calls 'another body', meaning the real and intimate one. Like Mama, the Maroons sealed their relationship with the living world through the body. Hence the fact that dreams, in this world, were very much *part of the ecology*, something which many Westerners find difficult to understand; they were part of the process of reconnecting the denied, repressed body to the environment. Marronage involves a whole system of incorporated knowledge; the same sort of system that operates in Congolin's herbalist practice.

I'm struck by how central dreams are to ideas of reciprocity between humans and other living beings in Jamaica, my homeland – and I'm also struck by how common this dynamic is among other communities around the globe, yet puzzled by how hard it is for Westerners to understand it. When I mention dreams and dreaming to my academic colleagues in England, the first go-to associations are Freud, Lacan and psychoanalysis, since so many Western-thinking minds can only view the unconscious through the lens of the 'subject', as they put it, a really Western way of understanding what it is to be a human being. But as the Nishnaabeg scholar Leanne Betasamosake Simpson explains in her book *As We Have Always Done*, dreams, in indigenous traditions, are part of the process of embedding yourself in the living ecology, in the web of all our relations, including plants and animals. She writes:

Nishnaabeg-Gikendaasowin, or Nishnaabeg knowledge, originates in the spiritual realm, coming to individuals through dreams, visions, and ceremony and through the process of gaa-izhi-zhaawendaagoziyaang – that which is given lovingly to us by the spirits. This makes sense because this is the place where our Ancestors reside, where spiritual beings exist, and where the spirits of living plants, animals, and humans interact.

Nobody needs to explain this to us where I'm from. It's so self-evident. So I can say the same thing about my Jamaican grung people, those who preserve the African lifeways of their ancestors in their bodies – like Mama, of course, and like Congolin.

It's a new morning, and I spend it writing. My neighbour Dwayne from downstairs at Miss Rita's has just come to offer me a huge bunch of bananas that he's cut down from the tree in the backyard. *Yeah man, a 'bout nine hand did de pon it,* he informs me, as I exult at its size. A few hours later, it's the afternoon, and I'm about to go have a shower when I hear Congolin calling, *Hol dog!* as he crosses the gradient that leads into the yard. His gait is something of a sashay mixed with a stumble. I notice again his permanently affixed smile. He's been walking for miles, with a rucksack slung over his shoulder. He takes it off as I come out to greet him. I invite him to take a seat on the veranda. *Come een no man, come siddung up yasso.*

I've hauled my pyjamas back on, ready to sit and chat with Congo. He's brought all sorts of foods and herbs for me. He reveals them one by one; I am jubilant. First a piece of bark from the breadnut tree. Then a cluster of a dried herb, which he reveals to be strong back. I lift it to my nostrils: the odour of horsehide mingled with the fragrance of newly turned soil, intertwined with hints of young cedar bark. *I no longer live close enough to the earth*, I reflect silently. What might my associations have been, if I still did? The herb exudes such a rich, musky scent that I want to keep sniffing it for days to come. I place it on my kitchen counter in a jute bag, which I open out so the herb can breathe and so that I can remember to inhale it occasionally.

I'm grateful that I have the richness of a food heritage that is still alive, visible, right before my eyes – and, indeed, under my nose. I'm grateful that living with the earth is not foreign to my being, that I'm not faced with the labour of learning it for the first time, and with a gulf of alienation. Certainly, what saddens me in Leeds is the distance from something I once knew, even as what excites me here in Jamaica is the ability to reconnect with the innocence of my childhood – a time when I relished the simple act of observation, attuned to the subtle shifts unfolding around me and keenly aware of their profound impact. Working with plants and understanding their power is understanding how the small things affect us and shape our destinies; it's revising our sense of human power and authority. What excites me here is that I did not grow up alienated from the land, that despite not having had a lot of it, my little family was still able to be connected to its power, to the life that happens around it. Given who I am, the likelihood that I would have had this opportunity in England, had I been born there, is slim. Thank goodness I know what it feels like to be connected to the source of what I consume.

There's a vigorous conversation happening in England around land access and equality, and around related concerns such as food justice and independence. Vigorous in certain quarters, even if one does not see or hear very much of it in the mainstream media. Tweets by Jon Moses, a freelance writer based in the UK, helped me to understand the urgency of this conversation, even as they brought home to me the salutary nature of my childhood, and just why I've been going back to it as a sort of refuge, faced with the land alienation I experience in Britain. Writing about the organised mass trespass of the 52,000-acre Badminton Estate in South Gloucestershire in the summer of 2022, the occasion that provided the context for his remarks, Moses notes:

> For the first time in many of the attendees' lives they were given the space, time and guidance to be intimate with the wildflowers which form part of our collective cultural inheritance but about which few of us know much about at all.
>
> It really drove home how deeply impoverished I – and we – really are. Not through idleness or choice but through dispossession and disempowerment.

This is a white British person speaking. He concludes:

> Trespassing is portrayed as an anti-social act. But who is really anti-social? The person who comes to reconnect with the land, or the people who took it away? Our countryside is choked under a militarised, misanthropic culture whose only language is barbed wire and Keep Out.

In *The Book of Trespass*, author Nick Hayes points out that in England, roughly fifty per cent of the land is owned by one per cent of its people. Interviewed for the BBC podcast series *My Albion*, in which the producer and narrator Zakia Sewell, a British woman of Carriacouan heritage, asks the question, *Do I belong to this land, and can this land belong to me?* (while going on a personal quest for the mythical Albion), Hayes reminds us that in many countries across Europe, including Scotland, the right of exclusive ownership of the land 'is seen as detrimental to the health of the nation, and as long as people treat the land with respect . . . and as long as you realise that you're there almost as a guest of nature, what the Scottish call "a responsible right to roam" is seen as a perfectly healthy aspect of your right to the land'. He laments the fact that what's considered a right in Scotland is considered a crime in England.

The phenomenon of enclosure in England has led to a situation in which engaging with wildflowers and the life of one's own land must now entail trespassing. In England, there are walls – physical ones – separating people from the earth. These walls are now so firmly erected in politics and in law that to imagine their dismantling is almost to dare to imagine the impossible. This is what writers like Jon Moses and Nick Hayes, and the Right to Roam Association, invite us to do – imagine the impossible. The website of the Right to Roam Association contextualises the issue in this way:

> In 2000, the Countryside & Rights of Way (CRoW) Act gave us a partial Right to Roam over about 8% of England. For the last two decades, we have had legal access to walk over certain landscapes (mountain, moor, commons and some downland, heath and coastlines) without fear of trespassing.
>
> But these sites are often remote, meaning that access to land has become a postcode lottery, available to those who live next to it, or who can afford the cost of travel and overnight stays. Everywhere else, not covered by the CRoW Act, the public are actively made to feel unwelcome in our own landscape and have been portrayed for centuries as a threat to the countryside.

Just stacking my kitchen counter at Miss Rita's helps me realise that the 'right to roam' issue is linked to food sovereignty. Ultimately, they are two sides of the same coin; they shine a light on an unjust and unsustainable land system that has threatened both human health and the health of the planet. Connecting with the land as kin and engaging with the foods we consume pedals our attention back to ways of knowing, being and interacting with the world that prioritise natural and cyclical processes.

On the veranda, Congolin takes out a transparent plastic bag full to bursting with carrots freshly harvested from his farm. Receiving all these foods from him is a rare kind of gratification. I start planning all the things I'll do with this amount of carrots – dumplings, juice, steamed carrots and okra with scallions and thyme. Then he unveils his powdered dandelion; I can see the brown-grey substance, which resembles black pepper, through another transparent plastic bag. A gift fit for a king, it will go back to England with me and join the stash of herbs I keep in one of my cupboards. From his rucksack, he also pulls out a two-quart bottle of carrot juice. *No water at all, just straight juice from the carrot, only ginger added.* We pour two big glasses. A light sting, a delicate scratch to the back of the throat, no bits, frothy and smooth. Then we simply sit there on the veranda, relaxed and happy, as he explains to me how to apply to my eyes the pure cannabis juice he's distilled and brought for me in a vial. I'm a bit sceptical. I am to use this in alternation with the whitish liquid from the flower buds of the African tulip tree – *waterman*, Congo calls it – to relieve the eye strain caused by spending too much time at the computer.

After about an hour spent on the veranda, I freshen up, get

dressed and gather my car keys. I'm taking him to Mandeville to purchase a phone. A small thing like this is something I can do as a gesture of thanks for all that he's given me – not just the physical things, but the wisdom, the grace. This morning, I'm enveloped in a profound sense of blessing, from the gestures of warmth and kindness that have been extended to me through my encounter with Congolin. I feel I've absorbed what it might have taken me years to learn from books – indeed, what I might never have learned at all in that way. I feel hugely privileged, and the purchase of a phone is a paltry thing in comparison.

The red soil, the colour of paprika, glistens under the midday sun, amid rocks that seem a sort of coral left on the top of this mountain. Their waters have long receded, though these still make their presence felt: I cannot get the ocean out of my mind, or escape the physical sense that it is near, although the closest coastline is tens of miles away, not to mention hours by transport. In Coffee Grove, on the hillside plot of the herbalist Congolin, I'm hundreds of feet above sea level, yet the idea that the ocean belongs here never ceases to press against my thoughts, and along with it a feeling of time contracting. The spread of rock amid the ochre soil is something that should belong to the world of art, that should have its place on famed canvases in museums. The resplendence of the red brings to mind the light in Giorgione's paintings. The brightness cast by the midday sun on the surface of the rocks is beatific. Here, now, is a moment of realisation: I want to talk about images that don't build upon existing knowledge of what is beautiful. I want to talk about the absolute worthiness of this beauty. Teju Cole declares, 'I do not want to be seduced by what is photographable'; I agree. I want, instead, to be absorbed by what people do not allow themselves to see – by the blind spots in our ideas of the beautiful.

5.

Archival Detective

I set out from Coffee Grove at the crack of dawn, the cool morning air still clinging to the shadows. On the winding mountain road, the pulse of anticipation pushes me forward. In under two hours, I arrive at the doorstep of Velma Pollard, Erna Brodber's sister and a literary luminary in her own right, who greets me with a warmth that belies the early hour. After a fleeting exchange with Velma, I assist Dr Brodber in loading her belongings into the rear of the RAV4. With the city now stirring to life, we navigate through labyrinthine streets before being swallowed by the dense morning traffic heading towards downtown Kingston. We're bound for the National Land Agency.

At the agency, the supervisor is hostile; the mere act of requesting a map feels like stepping into a boxing ring. I find myself feeling my way around my own question. I'm not even sure what I'm looking for, so I take cues from Dr Brodber, who's asking for maps of her own.

A cadastral map . . . Yes, I'd like to see cadastral maps of the area . . . Coffee Grove and Mount Pleasant . . .

What you know 'bout cadastral map? the supervisor shoots back before I can even complete my question. *Because you hear the lady asking for cadastral map, you asking for cadastral too . . . ?* Her head tilts in condescension, while her bespectacled gaze defies me to say something, *anything* that suggests I know what a cadastral map is.

Well, I'm interested in boundary lines. I want to see the names of people who owned land and what their boundaries were at any time in the early 1900s. I know a cadastral map will show me that, I pursue. No use being intimidated here or you'll make no headway. Truth be told, I'd literally never heard the word *cadastral* before Dr Brodber mentioned it, but I happen to know the meaning of *cadastre* in French, a language I learned in high school, right here in Jamaica. Surprising how knowledge of a foreign language can help you with English in a moment like this.

Well, you have to know what you want, she says, tapping energetically on the counter of the air-conditioned room. From behind the glass partition, we stare at countless filing cabinets and a table covered with large maps piled one on top of the other. *You tell me what you want and I can help you from there . . . It's mostly researchers who come asking for cadastral maps.*

My urge is to laugh, but I know better than to do this. Making a faux pas with this head of section who seems determined to put me to the test at every turn? I might as well kiss goodbye to my hopes of finding anything. She might just be helpful, I think to myself, if you answer calmly. *In fact, I am a researcher . . . miss* – an extra dose of politeness – *I've travelled all the way from England to access these maps . . .*

Her tone relaxes a little. She mutters something in a low voice to a young clerk, who disappears and re-emerges with a map marked simply 'Manchester' with the year 1950 on it. *Here you go,* he says. *No photos, but you can get black-and-white photocopies, if you order them.* Colour photocopies require a special procedure and that takes a few days. And, yes, I can have a colour copy of the entire map in one, but Lord have mercy, that haffi go through the commercial department and that's a whole different procedure. So the clerk informs me, gazing into the ceiling as if looking at something he alone can see. I opt for the quicker, less hasslesome option, which is the black-and-white photocopy. I pay the cashier first as the clerk accompanies me, carrying the map. Despite this, I can hardly contain my excitement; if only he knew the treasure that it represents to me. That said, he'll have seen researchers making 'huge discoveries' every day. But Coffee Grove and Mount Pleasant on a map! I hadn't even considered the notion before.

What I have before me is, indeed, a cadastral map. It's exciting and useful, sometimes hard to read. Names include Mount Pleasant (written in bold), 700 acres, and J. M. Mitchell. Was this the James Mitchell who also owned Pusey Hall Estate in Clarendon and Amity Hall in St Thomas? Also: Coffee Grove, 780 acres. I see written down the names of places I never dreamed of seeing on a map in an air-conditioned government agency in Kingston. Places like Stricklands, which, given our capacity for transforming words, I've always known as Trickland – a far more mischievous-sounding name. St Toolis, Redberry, Whitney Turn . . . these are the places where I walked, ran, played, when I went to live with Dwina in Porus. *Back a bush*, my high school classmates called them, and I was forced to agree. I had no idea they were on maps held in archives.

But that's the mindset you adopt when your history is marked by erasures. Growing up, attending high school and even university, we were deemed 'small' people because we toiled the earth. That's how society viewed us. And, gradually, I internalised that depiction, believing our corner of the world wasn't significant enough to be worthy of a map or to be recorded in historical archives. Maps were for important places, places that had history. Mandeville, the capital of my parish, had history; its colonial architecture proved it. So did Christiana and Spalding. Even Porus had some history – a railway station, a courthouse, churches from the eighteenth century built by the whites. All we had was the grung and the houses we erected around it. So, I find myself unexpectedly revering the documented history of these familiar places, as if it somehow confirms our presence in the broader story.

I need a magnifying glass to read the names of landowners and the names of a series of smaller holdings beside them. The size of the writing corresponds, basically, to the scale of the place: Mount Pleasant and Coffee Grove are written in larger letters, given their acreage; you have to look closely to see Stricklands, as it's tiny. But 'Trickland' is a place I now know to be *in* Coffee Grove: the map also shows how geography shifted over time as these lands were acquired in the nineteenth and twentieth centuries by a new set of people – white British legatees, illegitimate 'natural' children of colonists ('free coloureds'), the Black peasantry.

This map is from 1950. (Mama was thirty-one in 1950, and already living in Mount Pleasant.) Yet this map shows Mount Pleasant as owned by one person at that time. Could large-scale plantation agriculture have remained a phenomenon in this area as recently as that? All this was just the other day. As helpful as the map is, it only heightens my curiosity about how the layout of smallholdings in the settlement of Coffee Grove came to be what it is now. I'll have to take these names with me (J. M. Mitchell et al.) to the catalogues of deeds that exist, as Dr Brodber informs me, at the Jamaica Archives, the Island Record Office and the National Library of Jamaica. Nobody's ever sure which department has what.

At the National Library, things are a lot smoother, partly because several of the library staff recognise Dr Brodber, who's been the subject of a recent exhibition there. We're well received when we enter the reception area of the Special Collections Unit on the second floor. The clerks retreat to their desktop computers, their minds agile and adept at sifting through databases. Soon they vanish into the recesses of the stacked shelves lining the room's rear, resurfacing bearing maps and surveyance deeds dating back to the nineteenth century, each swathed in protective white paper.

A survey map from 1836 shows the Whitney Estate surveyed in relation to the Coffee Grove Estate. The map is the first tangible object on which I've seen the words 'Coffee Grove Estate', a concept that hadn't even crossed my mind until a few weeks earlier, when it surfaced in the database of the Centre for the Study of the Legacies of British Slavery, situated in University College London. I'd simply looked for Coffee Grove's altitude above sea level when the search engine returned, as part of its results, a webpage showing me data concerning the number of slaves living on the Coffee Grove Estate in the first decade of the nineteenth century. Something shifted, and all of a sudden, I was going back in my mind to my history lessons to see if I could retrieve any information I'd learned about coffee cultivation by the white planters in Jamaica. It was all nebulous. It was as if all the references I had to planters and overseers and great houses and the whole system of plantation estates in my country had to do with sugar. *Sugar was king . . . sugar was king* . . . was some kind of catchphrase circling in my mind – from my history lessons in Grade 7 – a catchphrase that set the tone for how I'd view slave labour and plantation agriculture in my country: I thought, basically, that it was totally organised around sugar. But this, of course, is very far from the truth; the slavery economy was never so singular. Discovering the information on the UCL website and now examining this survey map make me realise that coffee

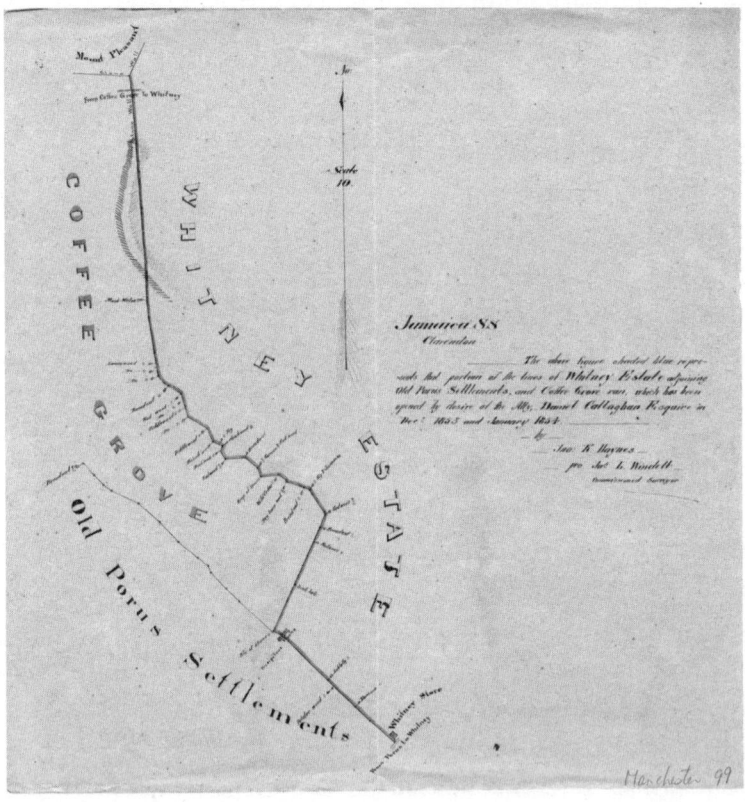

A survey map of Coffee Grove Estate showing the boundaries with the Whitney Estate as well as woodland, 1836. Courtesy of the National Library of Jamaica.

was very much a part of the story. Coffee and, in fact, trees and wood and plants.

The 1836 survey map was made at the height of commercial coffee cultivation in Jamaica: between 1800 and 1840, the island became one of the largest coffee producers in the world, yielding an estimated 70,000 tonnes of it per year. But, significantly, this map also documents the trees located on the plantation; they were clearly a precious resource: breadnut, redwood, wild cedar. Wood harvesting was an important part of the business of the estates. According to the logics of plantation ownership, acquiring land meant acquiring a set of rights that went along with it, including the right to its trees; it was simply one of the perks of property, valuable to the accumulation of wealth. It strikes me that I've never heard the names of some of these trees, like lancewood, fiddlewood and beefwood. Some may be known by other names here. Is 'redwood' an alternative name for the logwood? The logwood's a tree I wrote about in my poem of the same name, once I realised that this tree, so prevalent in my childhood memories of the commons with Mama, was also central to the dyestuffs industry in Leeds during the eighteenth and nineteenth centuries. The textile industry there consumed huge amounts of dyes from indigo and logwood originating in Jamaica and other colonised territories of the Americas. It may also be that some trees, like the damson and the birch, have disappeared from our entire Jamaican landscape, including Coffee Grove.

Pursuing my clues further, I'm now sitting downstairs in the main reading room of the library, where I leaf through the *List of Properties* published by the Geological Survey Department, which cover the first five decades of the twentieth century. These, while dealing with a relatively late period in Coffee Grove's history of coffee cultivation, nevertheless give precious insights into its larger history.

In the library's archive of coffee-related newspaper clippings, labelled 'Coffee 1900–1959', I stumble upon a headline from *Farmers Weekly*, a magazine aimed at the British farming industry. It's from 19 January 1959 and reads, laconically, 'World Coffee Problems'. It laments the global investor distrust in coffee. The recent International Coffee Agreement in Washington lacked provisions, it explains, to regulate surplus stock disposal or discourage overproduction. As in many of the newspaper clippings I peruse, this article testifies to a surge in global production of the coffee bean by the mid-twentieth century, resulting in increased competitiveness and a fall in prices – the collapse of the viability of a large-scale coffee economy in Jamaica. A far cry from the reign of coffee houses in London and the trade in coffee that thrived until the second half of the nineteenth century. By the end of that century, the importance of coffee houses in the metropolises of Britain had drastically diminished, a phenomenon that had repercussions for the coffee industry in the colonies. Besides, in the decades following the abolition of slavery in 1834, the coffee industry in Jamaica had already struggled to increase its export yields. By the middle of the twentieth century, many of the estate holders in my part of Jamaica, including Coffee Grove, had abandoned coffee cultivation, divesting their holdings and, in the process, drastically rearranging the region's economy. What was also drastically transformed was the lay of the land and its use, since it was the selling out of the coffee-estate lands as freeholdings to peasants that permitted so many of us to come into possession of them. In his book *Free Jamaica 1838– 1865: An Economic History*, the historian Douglas Hall writes:

As the cane-fields retreated and as the coffee planters moved from one eroded mountain slope to begin their ruin of another, the emancipated negroes and coloured people swarmed in search of freeholds, buying up the ruined acres of abandoned estates and the less accessible runs of still virgin estate land which were suitable for market-gardening.

This brings me back to my great-grandmother, Ma Minky, and her migration from Ellen Street to Mount Pleasant in the late nineteenth century. This is how Joe Morgan's clan came to own land, quite a bit of it, I've been told, before he sold the bulk of it off piecemeal in the latter part of his life as things got difficult financially. All of that is to say that Douglas Hall's observations also bring me back to Mama, as these are the conditions that made for my existence: Mama falling upon Joe Morgan, settling down with him, eventually separating from him, without divorcing – the Church of God forbade that; you lived alone for the rest of your life – before moving down to Coffee Grove, a single Black peasant woman, to purchase land in the district.

The list of properties compiled by the Department of Collections between 1910 and 1930 details their respective uses. Each time, Coffee Grove and Mount Pleasant are listed as 'ruinate' (sometimes 'grazing'). I wonder out loud what this could be. Sister Erna, who sits opposite me, thinks that 'ruinate' refers to land that had once been cleared for the purpose of agricultural cultivation, but which subsequently lapsed back into 'bush'. Such land includes soils that had been impoverished or eroded. 'Ruinate' seems to show up much more often after the large-scale cultivation of coffee ended.

This period witnessed, then, an important transfer that would progressively change the face of the land. By the time my mother was born in 1959, there would be far fewer English and Scottish men and women running coffee estates, and far more Black peasants carrying out small, independent farming. Coffee would continue to be important, since families would use pre-industrial peasant methods to produce it, selling much of their crop to the Coffee Industry Board, a central authority created in 1950 by the planter class, which effectively still ran the country. This supply was a very tiny drop in the ocean of the ever-expanding, worldwide demand for coffee, but for the peasants, whom hardly anybody ever asks to tell their story, this sort of cultivation was good enough. It was peasant time; it was the time of the small people.

I do remember Mama being the secretary of the local Coffee Board. It seems she'd occupied this role since long before I was born. Opposite our small house stood a barbecue, our name for the flat stone structure on which coffee is washed and dried. On the days when coffee was collected, this was a place of hectic activity. Peasant farmers would carry their coffee here to be weighed and recorded by the men in trucks sent by the government-owned processing facilities, before collecting payment. Later, at the end of the trading season, each coffee cultivator would be paid dividends based on the profits the Coffee Board had made on the year's overall harvest. But when peasants have control of the land, independence becomes the order of the day. They use the land for their own economies, for their own needs. This is how Coffee Grove, this rocky mountain district abandoned by the coffee estates and their British planters, became yam country.

The archives at the National Library have given me so

much precious insight into this history, but they've also left me with many questions: When did this transition begin to happen? What took place here in the immediate aftermath of emancipation? When did the colonists begin to sell the land and when did the peasants start to acquire it? And how? And who exactly were these peasants – how can I find out more about them? And another major question: Who was the British planter who established the Coffee Grove Estate? At library closing time, I say goodbye to Dr Brodber with these questions swirling in my head. I check into one of Kingston's nicer hotels for the night. When I arrive at the Jamaica Archives the next morning, I hardly expect to uncover any answers to my enquiries. It's funny – you formulate questions about the history you know is hiding in plain sight and yet when you do stumble on answers, you're caught off guard, unprepared for the discoveries.

To get to the archives, I drive half an hour into the centre of the historical quarter of Spanish Town, the old capital of Jamaica when the Spaniards colonised the island. The archives are in one of the centuries-old red-brick buildings, where Miss Williams, the Reading Room supervisor, welcomes me. I fill out forms, making very tentative requests that I hope may reveal something interesting about how Coffee Grove came into existence. Miss Williams suggests I look in the catalogues of crop returns and conveyances and disappears behind metallic silver doors, re-emerging with a few large and heavy leather-bound catalogues. Some of these are more than two centuries old.

It's in the crop returns that I make a major discovery, perhaps the biggest discovery from this trip to Kingston. A return from 1832 – the year preceding the passing of the

Abolition of Slavery Act – reveals that in February of that year, there were 116 enslaved people registered on the Coffee Grove Estate. Up to this time, the plantation was managed by an attorney, Duncan Robertson, on behalf of the heirs of one David Hutchison of Ayr in Scotland. David Hutchison, I discover with Miss Williams's help, died in 1820 in Black River, St Elizabeth, which is very near to Parottee, the district that Mama was originally from.

But the first time we actually see David Hutchison in the archive is the year 1797, when 300 acres of land were granted to him by George III 'of Great Britain, France and Ireland King and of Jamaica Lord Defender of the Faith', via letters patent from Alexander Lindsay, 6th Earl of Balcarres, the Lieutenant Governor of the Island of Jamaica. In the letters patent, we are told that David 'hath transferred himself with his servants and slaves into our beloved island in pursuance of a Proclamation made in the reign of his late Majesty King Charles the second . . . to become one of our planters there and for divers other Causes and Considerations'. As the first available crop records show, the lands in question had been designated as 'Coffee Grove'. According to the letters patent, these lands were situated in the parish of Vere. While Coffee Grove is now located in Manchester, it's worth noting that Manchester was formed from portions of Vere and two neighbouring parishes, Clarendon and St Elizabeth, in 1814. This is the origin of my district: I've found it here in officialdom, in a two-hundred-and-something-year-old leather-bound volume of deeds in the Jamaica Archives.

I've read in the work of historian David Austin that by the 1760s, roughly a third of the white population of Jamaica were Scots. Even today, many of the most common surnames in

Jamaica are Scottish clan names: Gordon, Davis, Douglas, Forbes, Graham, Murray . . . Our captive forebears had the names of their white masters imposed on them – another act of erasure. Many of these enslavers were Highland peoples who were themselves victims of English colonisation in their own lands. Yet, by getting involved in this 'English sugar island' (as it was then called) in the Caribbean, they were now making huge fortunes off the forced labour of kidnapped Africans.

It's already noon and I've been here since the place opened at 9 a.m. I know I'm hungry, but I can't spare a moment to stop and eat; I'm tripping on excitement. I need to go back to Coffee Grove this evening, and time in the archives moves too quickly. Where do I go from here, and how do I find out more about David Hutchison? Miss Williams informs me that the Island Record Office is only a ten-minute drive away, at a place called Twickenham Park, where they store deeds, conveyances, wills. There, she says, I might be able to find out more about David and what he did with his lands.

I bob and weave through the mad afternoon traffic, jumping a few queues and also pushing my way through when other drivers decide to do the same – real Jamaican stylee. When I make it to the Island Record Office, breathing heavily, they mercifully accommodate the researcher who's come all the way from England. Mr Reynolds, the archivist, allows me to skim through mountains of deeds and wills. I start by searching catalogues from the twentieth century, using the names of people I know, but I soon realise that I'll make little progress this way: the peasants didn't register their properties; in fact, like Mommy, like Mama, many of them still don't – all they have is common-law titles. While I'm pondering, Mr Reynolds appears at my desk. *Why don't you look among the wills that we have here?* he suggests. *If you can find David's will, you should be able to see who inherited his property and what they did with it.* Sound reasoning: if I can find the identities of David's successors, I might be able to establish a chain of land ownership. I search the will catalogues until closing time. Desperate and frustrated, I accept the fact that I'll have to pay for another night at the hotel in Kingston and return to the Island Record Office tomorrow. Thankfully, the next day does bring joy, precisely the kind of joy I was hoping for: with Mr Reynolds' help, I eventually locate the listing of David's last will and testament in a catalogue. Soon Mr Reynolds emerges from the holy vaults bearing a dusty and enormous leather tome filled with endless calligraphic cursive that I have to train myself to decipher. Slowly, I start to make sense of David's will. It opens with the following words:

I, David Hutchison, of the Parish of Manchester, planter, bequeath all my plantation in Manchester called Coffee Grove together with slaves and stock to my beloved brother, George Hutchison, of the City of Edinburgh in Great Britain and to Alex Moore, Esq., of St Elizabeth in trust for the purposes hereinafter recited.

George, the above-mentioned brother, is one of David's inheritors – £1,000, a significant sum of money at the time – and so are David's 'beloved sister', Agnes Jean Hutchison of London; Agnes's son, George Ferguson Hutchison; and one Miss Jean Hutchison of Ayr, 'daughter of the late provost, James Hutchison', presumably a close relation. David had no 'legitimate' children. Instead, his will lists 'five reputed children by Elizabeth Hunt, a free woman of colour'. Incidentally, all five children, aged three to fourteen, were baptised at Elgin, Scotland, in 1820, the year of their father's death. In the will, they each receive '£100 at the time of [David's] death, then £200, then £1000 each when they attain 21 years'. David made good provision for these 'natural' children of his: in addition to the financial bequests, his will stipulates that 'A comfortable dwelling house is to be erected and furnished on Coffee Grove for Miss Hunt and her children and they are to have to services [*sic*] of 8 slaves'. A further twist is that archival records list David's daughter Jean, this child of 'a free woman of colour', as an unsuccessful claimant for 'slave compensation for Coffee Grove estate in Manchester, Jamaica, as one of the residuary legatees of her father David Hutchison'. The slave compensation in question was the one given by the British government to the owners of slaves by an Act of Parliament, the Slave Compensation Act of 1837, for the loss of their 'property' upon emancipation. The package was £20 million at the time, which several estimates put at around £87 billion in today's money. It was so huge that British taxpayers – in other words, many of the readers of this book – were still paying for it until 2015.

I'm here in Jamaica as I make these discoveries, but they help me understand, with such immediacy, just how the spoils of slavery provided the sort of wealth that would consolidate large-scale land ownership in Britain, the money being used to purchase huge swathes of these isles. It is this magnate land ownership that would speed up the erasure of common land in the British Isles, as regular people were evicted from the land they had lived with for centuries. I see now that this radical alteration in the relationship between regular people and the land in Britain – and this includes the Highland Clearances in Scotland, David Hutchison's country – is integrally linked to slavery in places like Jamaica. I am seeing that the profits of slavery and the repercussions of land injustice in Britain today are directly linked.

The profits of slavery were crucial in establishing and consolidating what we might call 'land power' in Britain as we know it today. The expropriation and forcible enclosure of vast amounts of land for the creation of large pastoral farms and game-hunting reserves, the attendant impoverishment of rural communities, the eviction of tenants in the Highland Clearances, and post-famine emigration to Australia, Canada, New Zealand and the West Indies, among other related phenomena, are all linked to the wealth amassed from slavery in the West Indian colonies in the eighteenth and nineteenth centuries. In her extensively researched work *Our Island Stories*, Corinne Fowler notes how 'land purchases in the Highlands and Islands doubled in the 1830s, when slave-owners were compensated for lost slave labour following the 1833 Slavery Abolition Act', adding that 'forty per cent of these lands were bought after compensation money was claimed by those who owned or inherited plantations.' As she also notes, some Highland landlords receiving compensation payouts from the British government for the emancipation of their slaves had never even set foot in the West Indies.

Of all the characters in this story, it's David's youngest child, James, who commands my immediate attention. Born in December 1817, James died at ninety-nine years old in 1917 as a married pen-keeper 'at Farenough in Manchester'. *Farenough* . . . Far enough? Is this the *Faranuff* that Mommy took me to see only a few days ago? I know history will ultimately hold on to many of Faranuff's secrets, but I am convinced that this place Farenough, mentioned in David Hutchison's will, has to be the Faranuff that we know now. How could it be coincidental?

Mr Reynolds and I mention James's name so often that he starts to become a character in a story we're both desperate to tell. It feels like James is the key to unlocking so much history. Unfortunately, our research comes to a standstill since James's will, which is listed among the records held in the archive – I get so excited when I see this – is not on-site and Mr Reynolds has to request it. I can hardly wait to see what turns up. I know I've only skimmed the surface.

But around four days after returning to Coffee Grove, I open my emails one afternoon and see a message from Mr Reynolds:

Good day,

Apologies for the delayed response; however unfortunately, the given record has been listed as destroyed and cannot be reproduced. I am sorry for any inconvenience this may have caused.

You're not as sorry as I am, Mr Reynolds, that's for sure.

How can this be? Why was I brought so close, shown the door of entry, as it were, only to have my hopes dashed? Where do I look now? I will continue, for sure. I don't know how long it will take me, or if I'll ever find anything, but I promise the ancestors that I'll keep on searching: the National Archives at Kew Gardens, the British Library . . . wherever I can possibly look.

★

The expanse of time between this place now and its slavery-era history is like the daunting chasm between two colossal rocks that one wishes to get over. Aren't James's genes still in the blood of some of the people living in Coffee Grove and Mount Pleasant? I am reminded of some lines I wrote in a prose poem: 'Without any witness (writing, inscriptions, books, legends) tying that time to the present, all the stories have to be invented.' Of course, we do have some writing – the archival traces of David Hutchison are one valuable kind – but making the connections in our history, which for so long was told by the colonists rather than by ourselves, is always such arduous work. How do we tell the stories that are there and not there at the same time?

Missing history:
Allowing it to be seen hiding . . .

perhaps the closest we come to recording it.

6.

The Poetry of Monuments

It's around 7.30 a.m. when I've finished making lunch and having breakfast. Soon I'm outside, clad in my water boots, mainly as a precaution against ticks and grass lice that might sneak up my trousers as I venture through the tall grass. Unlike my recent trip to Faranuff with Mommy, when we drove up to Mount Pleasant, today I want to recreate the regular journey Mama and I took to the Post Office; I'm going on foot and I'm going alone. With my backpack slung over my shoulders, containing my camera, lenses and a home-made lunch, I set off on the mile-and-a-half trek.

Under the morning sun, the cabbages gleam, lush and inviting. The sun, still gentle at 8 a.m., casts a tolerable warmth as I stroll along the road, inhaling the earthy blend of vegetal scents – deep chlorophyll, resin and the fragrance of surrounding barks. This road holds a history intertwined with my life, ancestral and personal memories of traversing vast distances on foot. My people are a walking people, a legacy that stretches back to the arduous journeys endured by those captives sold to the slave ships. Here, however, I reflect on the countless miles my forebears and I have trodden over these hills.

Mommy's daily five-mile trek from Coffee Grove to Bellefield for school, followed by the additional journey to Mandeville, devoured hours of her day, leaving scant time for school friendships. By the time I reached primary school age, I had moved in with her in Porus and I escaped the arduous daily journey, but suffered the emotional toll of separation from Mama – a separation whose impact I've only recently begun to articulate.

When I started travelling the Coffee Grove road, or rather, when Mama started carrying me along that road, it was not paved. It was simply stone and rock, red dirt gleaming under the sun, with dirt tracks branching off like the tentacles of some insect, wriggly tracks leading to wood or wattle-and-daub houses perched on stilts. Along the red dirt road were numerous cultivation patches and countless farmers tilling them, patches of potato slips and cabbages, hillocks of yams, coco and dasheen. In the yam vines that form a thick, rich foliage, you have never seen a green so deep, so succulent. Abundance. Throw a rotting tomato in your backyard this evening and watch tomato suckers spring up by morning.

Last night, I saw in my dream a hairpin bend in the road, a bend forming the beginning of a steep incline. Simply an image that peers out of the folds of the mind and comes alive in the flesh. It was a humble bend, wide and deep. It's a real bend that exists on this road. Its image recurs in my dreams, etched into my memory by its sharpness and significance as the threshold to the most daunting ascent of the journey. So many things are insurmountable when you're four years old. But it's the humbleness that strikes me about the bend of that time. Humble, the red dirt, the dirt that was, as I would find out, a sign of the presence of bauxite. How it leaves a streak on everything, on the stones, on the grass, at the base of the trees. And those red streaks, ubiquitous in our mountainside villages, became the mark of lowliness – smallness. I felt it must have been so in everybody else's mind; it felt obvious.

I had never noticed the streaks before I went to high school. I notice them again now. At primary school, there was no need to notice them. Most of us were from red dirt. Red bauxite dirt. It was everywhere in our yards. We white-washed the trees to hide it. All of us knew red dirt. My high school friends who bought their box lunches from the shop across the street fancied they were better than the dirt. I had never before formulated the thought that some people were better, higher. But it was in that bauxite dirt that we played marbles, got our uniforms red.

I notice the dirt now, how it was humble and homely and everything I knew. And Mama, carrying me up the hill to Mount Pleasant every weekday morning, the steep hill where she had to lift me up. Because nobody had cars then, a trip to Kingston meant going down the dreaded Jokoto Hill; even the name, with those three staccato syllables, and the three *o*'s suggesting infinity – even the name invokes terror. In a way, there were two roads into and out of Coffee Grove, the mildly tolerable one, which had and still has no name, but which one might refer to as *the road to Blue Mountain* – not to be confused with the famed coffee-growing mountain range in the east – and Jokoto Hill, symbol of our terribleness and our daily ability to master it.

Back then, when a vehicle did appear, heads popped out of windows and neighbours rushed to their verandas to catch a glimpse. I doubt they do any more – there must be a lot of cars passing nowadays.

In those days of rough, unpaved roads, the mere thought of coaxing a taxi driver to brave the journey to Coffee Grove with your market goods and hamper seemed outlandish. The question wouldn't even surface in your imagination.

Your imaginary was walking, carrying, distances. Why would the driver come when there was no road? When he'd have to drive miles to find even one passenger to take back in the opposite direction? Taxis came only rarely, often for special occasions like Sister Nez's arrival from the airport, heralded by honking and fanfare but no stop at our house. It was as if some perverse game was being played out, leaving Mama to call out in vain as the vehicle rushed past, leaving dust in its wake.

Cars, it seemed, only arrived carrying people from foreign lands, or for graduations. Few other journeys were made on the unpaved road, which remained red dirt until I was around eight or nine. The paving process took about two years to cover the three-mile stretch. Before the road was asphalted, villagers would don their best shoes after washing their feet at the standpipe before entering the nearby towns – Porus, Christiana, Spalding, Mandeville – with their more 'respectable' roads. Now, I reflect on those rocks tinged with crimson ore, the dirt that leaves an indelible stain on memory.

I have often stood for a while looking down into a dirt track that leads into somebody's yard in Coffee Grove, or down to somebody's grung. The redness of the track contrasts with the rain-drenched greenness of the shrubs along the way, and the track sneaks off interminably, as these tracks do. It feels strange to admit it, but I was often ashamed to say that I came from here. And after a while, when it occurred to me to take photos to 'preserve' my memories – when Mama died, in 2012, I must have felt that other things were dying – I felt ashamed to share them with friends. So many of my friends are worldly; I felt I would hurt them by subjecting them to these images. Certainly, this was about not wanting to hurt them, but also about not hurting their image of me.

I feel silly now to have to admit that I was ashamed of the yam vines. All that green – so deep, there almost seems to be a hint of blue beneath it. All that devastating, merciless lushness, all that growth, all that bounty from the earth to nourish us. The earth. The stuff that uptown Kingstonians went to Coronation Market to get – and they'd be proud to do this, connecting with their roots – was grown by people like Mama. And yet I was ashamed.

As I stand gazing at the track, it feels as though it foreshadows a journey I was destined to undertake. Observing the dirt path now, I reflect that back then, I sensed the existence of another version of myself, inhabiting a different time, with a completely distinct perspective on this very track. It felt like a departure from the village, yet simultaneously an immersion into its essence.

Memory is most intense when it becomes physical, and the tangible relics of the past awaken powerful sensations in ways that defy words – because these remnants render the past present. So it is with the lost places of our childhood that we revisit. The placing of our feet on an old set of stones we remember, walking the land we half remember, the viewing of a landscape that's different but the same – we can perceive the former landscape just below it. In such moments, memory is vivid, overwhelming even, yet always barely beyond reach – this is when it's most powerful, because it haunts us, and what haunts us is, by definition, existing and yet untouchable. Memory is like this – the physical sensation of something absent. We build monuments, we gather things in chambers and storage spaces, we gather relics into our inner world the way the people here gather stones. Each moment is part of an amassing, a pulling together.

The act of writing also embodies this process. I write to preserve the dead. Today I want to bring one more moment into my trove of gathered memories, another stone to a heap of stones – akin to the ones I see gathered like burial cairns in the middle of the fields along the road. In these fields, hills of yams topped with lush vines running up their supporting bamboo sticks intermingle with white mounds of rock, and among these mounds there are clearings in which new food crops will be planted: scallions, thyme, sweet potatoes, cabbages, ginger. As I think about the process of remembering, I can't help but feel that this practice of gathering rocks into mounds has something similar to it. Memory is an intentional act of collecting disparate things, of heaping them up. The French word for contemplation or reverence is *recueillement*, which literally means 'a gathering again of things'. A re-collection. That's probably the significance of the rocks in an atavistic sense. Perhaps they themselves carry memory, and the practice of gathering and heaping suggests an act of care. Perhaps it involves a gesture we've become unfamiliar with: heaping things up, gathering fragmented pieces, again.

The once rugged path is now smoothed by pavement. I begin my ascent. A mile or so after leaving Miss Rita's, I near the common where Mama and I would turn off. In this common, there used to be a track leading almost directly to the Post Office, cutting out a good half a mile of road. Hesitant, I gaze into the common, unsure if the path still exists. A man, perched where the hill slopes, catches my uncertainty. With a nod towards the cultivation grung he's just emerged from, he gestures: *A tru de so . . . yeah man, you can walk tru de.* His gait resides indelibly in my memory, so does his face and the sense of the cutlass hanging loosely from his hand the way it does now, though I can't remember a single thing about him beyond this meeting of body and place: not who his family is; not the things we used to say to each other when I was a mere child and he a teenager carrying around a cutlass wherever he went, an appendage to his body; not his name, which he reminds me now is Floyd.

My purpose is clear – to rediscover the path Mama and I once took to reach the postal agency. It wound its way through lands owned by one of those peasant landowning dynasties like the Parkinsons, Peddys and Martins of Coffee Grove – large areas of tillage and pasture for grazing. The pathway snaked along the edges of the swathe and eventually through it. At the edge of this expanse of grung, it became a ribbon tucked between the yards of the families who possessed the land. Their names and faces are now lost to me, but, astonishingly, the pathway remains unchanged, tracing the same route it did thirty, forty years ago. Floyd was right – *Yeah man, it de-de man* [meaning, the path], *but it bush up . . . you a wear the right shoes.* I'm wearing calf-high water boots, and I reckon the only thing needed to complete my farmer look is a cutlass; I am instead, however, carrying my SLR camera, which makes me stand out somewhat, in any case, as *probably a foreigner*, though not one who couldn't have originally come from here.

As I follow the path to Mount Pleasant, I'm struck by the enduring constancy of my childhood surroundings. The familiar *cut-through road*, though unofficial, is still here, a communal artery connecting the village. It's still *a road* that everyone can use. It runs through people's 'property', but no one will complain; no one will forbid me from taking this track by saying something like: *Hello, I'm afraid this is private property!* Or something more aggressive, like: *What are you doing?! You can't be here . . . !* I'm doing nothing illegal because even if there's some law on the books that refers to crossing over into someone's 'property', the sense of commonwealth that exists here prevents what I'm doing from being considered *trespassing.*

Suddenly I am walking here again at five, six, seven years old, eight possibly, even nine, going up to Mount Pleasant to the postal agency, where I will stay all day, playing or entertaining myself by forming letters and writing words; where I'll read stories. *Run, Dick, run. See Dick run. Jack runs to get the ball. See Jane go. Jane . . . The dog called Spot.* In my reading primer, blond white children run after a ball on a lawn bordered by a neat, low picket fence. And those Bible stories . . . Jesus, the disciples, Moses and Pharaoh . . .

I see myself at three years old doing the whole uphill climb with Mama to 'Post Office', as people call the little agency. But it was long for my little feet. I must've been heavy for Mama by that time. Imagine her carrying me every day, in her arms, on her back. A heavy baby. No choice. All love. No questions. Hard life. Joy and love. How did she manage this weight that I was on her ageing body? Up the hill, through the fields, among the cows, the gaulins perched on their backs, over the bumblebees tunnelling the dung. The daily rhythm of walking and saying good morning to everyone, to the man working his field, to the woman cooking the pot, to the children going to school. The heat, and the little boy sweating, complaining, *Mama, I can hardly go . . .* The little boy crying inexplicably. Mama not knowing what to do any more. Mama discovering a fattened tick between big toe and long toe in the night. Poor child. What a mama. At sixty-two years old.

In the common this morning, there's an absence of cattle adorned with gaulins, and Mama isn't here guiding us past the grazing bull. It's the same scarlet earth, however, and my water boots are progressively becoming Coffee Grove boots, slowly taking on the life of the ground. I see myself as a picture – a strange man with a camera slung over his shoulder, a jute bag in his hand and water boots on his feet. A certain familiarity is suggested, but he's not from here. Who is he?

Allow me to break one of you; thank you for your permission. These words I address to a patch of flowers that blanket the expanse before me. *I seek to know you intimately, to understand your secrets.* Enchanting and alluring, and at the same time forbidding; their stalks grow tightly packed and tall, producing, some distance from their tips, a perfect orb of prickles. Within me stir fleeting recollections of childhood escapades with my friend Damion, Maas Owen's son, the thrill of wild runs through Coffee Grove's commons, where the bachelor buttons snagged at our clothes like eager fingertips grasping for a world beyond theirs. Beside the floral blanket, a meticulously tended bed of tomatoes cascades down a gentle slope, the rich earth nourishing its vibrant hues.

As I take the final slope that leads me on to the Mount Pleasant road, I'm increasingly eager to see the little postal agency, the reason I used to come here at all. If something in me intensifies as I get closer to the place of the Post Office – a longing, a memory, a sense of familiar place – mustn't it be because I'm getting closer also, in a certain way, to Mama? It seems I could hardly ever separate Coffee Grove and Mount Pleasant from her. All my experiences of this place involve this elderly woman who ran the Post Office. But will the Post Office still be there? Will the ground have been given up to another building, to an entirely different activity, like farming? Will I even be able to identify the spot on which the little structure stood? I can't bear the thought of not being able to see the Post Office at least one last time.

Arriving at the main road, I'm greeted by a flurry of familiar faces and by voices emanating from people seated or standing at one of the shops lining the street. Each encounter, a trip down memory lane. Here, amidst the bustle of life, I am simply Tommy once more, no more and no less. *Sister Morgan Tommy*, they call me. With each exchange, the same incredulous refrain: *Tommy?! Me can't believe say a the little bwoy what Sta Morgan used to have a carry come a Post Office.* Their astonishment at my presence here, now, is almost tangible. It's as if I've emerged from the mists of time, resurrected in flesh and blood. Their words are a validation of my existence in this realm of shared memories. *Little Tommy . . . you turn big man . . . You a walk and look.* You're still walking these streets, they marvel. In their eyes, I am a living testament to the passage of time.

Within twenty minutes, I'm there, standing at the stone-wall entrance, looking at the weeds in the yard. I consider the back of this little edifice, the former postal agency, overgrown with its lianas. I take in the wattle-and-daub construction, the structure no larger than three metres by three. A perfect, comical square. How laughable it is to call this small, one-room shack a post office. *Stop doing that thing*, I scold myself. *What if you adopted the mindset you had when you were five? What if you tried to see this place through your five-year-old eyes? What would be so bad about that?* So much of this moment in time is about the possibility of becoming a child again, the possibility of accessing the kind of tenderness that childhood promises, that it – mine, certainly – does indeed allow. The tender sensuality of the world's touch, the feel of things on one's skin, along with, of course, the touch of parents – in my case, of my grandmother, Mama. After all, the tenderness of the touch of a leaf, of dirt on the hands, of grass against feet, of a grove or arbour that enfolds you, is so evocative of the foetal home. This is about installing myself, fiercely, into that tenderness that had been denied me for so long; it's thinking about how my people have been denied this tenderness for so long – about how a system works to deny them this. This, ultimately, is what this new first experience of the world is about.

I've slept in university dormitory rooms larger than this, I reflect silently. It's a hodgepodge kind of construction. I refrain from calling it Frankensteinian; that's too disdainful. I'm ashamed that 'Frankensteinian' is the best description I can conjure for what might be the second most important building in my life, after Mama's house. The thought crosses my mind as I note the wattle-and-daub sides and front, juxtaposed with the concrete back so crudely plastered that I can make out the lines where the stacked breeze blocks meet each other. A piece of board protrudes from the back of the roof, and I notice for the first time how rough the roofing is, so rough that the construction takes on a makeshift quality. That slight piece of wood at the back, some kind of cross-beam, lies underneath a wooden pole that's as natural in its shape – uneven and slightly undulating – as the moment it was cut from some nearby tree. *Must be good wood, the kind that doesn't rot,* I muse. I notice for the first time the other four poles running along the length – which is also the width – of the former postal agency.

The roof is a single layer of zinc nailed to thin pieces of wood that lie between it and the poles. How did the water not enter every time it rained? As for the awning, it's made of sheets of zinc lying on top of a mixture of planks and poles held up by two solid but weather-beaten wooden columns. Roughshod. Perhaps the individual materials are extremely resistant – mahogany or lignum vitae? *There's some miracle at work here,* I think to myself, *that has kept this roof intact.* Just now at the bar, an old friend spoke about how this little roof has survived every hurricane since our childhood while numerous others, modern ones, had been blown off by successive storms. Now I am incredulous at seeing the building still standing, as if in a time bubble, the same way it was the last time I was here twenty-five years ago. I look for the secret to the mystery of the building's longevity, its resistance to the deadliest storms, its secret congruity. For whatever that mystery is, it impresses me.

The parcel scale lying atop an old cast-iron safe is barely rusted, despite the length of time since this place fell into disuse. I can still make out the bureaucratic teal of the safe, recalling that much of the postal paraphernalia, from the postman's satchel to the postmistress's seal, was this colour.

The scale still lies there, as if it was 1985 and Mama was about to open up the agency and start weighing the parcels that Postman would soon deliver. I'd remembered nothing about this stuff. I remain at a cautious distance to peer inside, wary of going too close to the cast-iron burglar bars where wasps have formed nests; they've also nested all along the edges of the roof.

I am fascinated by the *turn-yuh-hand-make-fashion*, the rough technology, of my people. I'm intrigued by their particular way of making things work. I can't put my finger on it, but there's a beauty in this roughness that I need to figure out. I observe for the first time the artistry of clay or mud constructions, whose popularity in Jamaica had been waning by the time I was a child. I'd always just summed up this kind of construction as *poor people kinda house*, but I realise that, as with most things *poor people kind*, there's a craft, a deftness.

Vague memories stir of playing here, upon, around and among these rocks. It surprises me now that as a child I learned to play and find security, even joy, among them. Their rugged crevices, sharp edges, and hollows reminiscent of crustacean shells or hidden fish lairs were my playground. I learned to be at home here, on this rocky terrain. Consider this ground, with its jutting, jagged contours – a terrible beauty – a daunting landscape on which I learned to be safe. To live with insecurity is to learn to make one's home upon rough surfaces. Their beautiful roughness.

So you come back . . . A young man crosses the street to call to me. I'm still standing in the yard of the Post Office. As with most people, I must retrace a mental map of the years to arrive at his identity. The face is familiar, very familiar. *He must be my age* – how does one know such things, except that one just knows? His arms are sculpted by sinewy muscles. *Yeah man*, I reply as I walk to meet him, *deh ya a relive the old days*. I need to just keep talking and see if I catch the voice. It's Damion, my playmate from back then.

You talk same way, eeh man? I can feel Damion's unhurried inspection, his eyes slowly scanning me from top to bottom. Being a foreigner involves speaking with a little twang. Short of a little accent, people might consider that you're not foreign enough. To be foreign is to be 'doing well'. That's how it's always been round here, since my time and before.

Damion and I talk about what has changed and what has remained more or less the same. He tells me he works a variety of jobs. Right now, he's wearing steel-toe construction boots; he's just taken a break from some building happening over at the church to talk to the 'somebody' that his brother told him he needed to come see. At other times, he can be found farming his little square of land. For now, he can continue to make a small living from this and feed his family, but he also shares with me his anxieties about the bauxite companies – for him, an ever-present threat. He waves his hand to indicate the expanse of land we can see in the distance, part of the old Whitney Estate (which may once even have encompassed Mount Pleasant). It's near the Post Office, even nearer to where my mother and I stood listening to the stream and talking about the sinkhole where the little boy Eulie had crouched so many decades ago. *The whole of before you ya-so a fi bauxite now* – all of that wide valley and the hill that rises above it now belong to a Chinese-owned bauxite company, he tells me. *You don't want them start mining ya-so enuh, cause if them start, everything mash up*, I say, trying to measure the scale of what would be lost. *The pollution*, he adds. *All them plant-ya wouldn't survive*, he remarks, pointing to the thriving biomass in the wild gardens in the yards opposite the Post Office. *Pollution and sickness.*

A *New York Times* article of 28 September 1974 notes that 'Jamaica is the second-largest producer in the world, after

Australia, of bauxite from which aluminum is made'. This remained the case for decades, before the bauxite companies began withdrawing from the country in the early 2000s, once their primary mining reserves had been depleted. This shift coincided closely with the unsettling news that Coffee Grove and Mount Pleasant were to be mined and the villagers uprooted and relocated. Now, twenty years later, the government has made new deals, this time with Chinese mining companies, who even drew up plans to mine within the Cockpit Country, the most ecologically sensitive part of Jamaica. (Mount Pleasant is located near its southern tip.) Lately, under pressure from a national outcry, the government has created a so-called 'protected area' within the Cockpit Country and has promised that no mining will take place within its boundaries, and the Supreme Court has also intervened with an order barring further mining of lands in this sensitive area.

I often think to myself, *how different these districts would have looked today, if mining plans had gone ahead.* Another natural economy would have been disrupted. Coffee Grove and Mount Pleasant would no longer be villages in which many continue to make an independent living from the soil. To see my people lose this vital and ordinary relationship with the land would have filled me with suffering. I'm often angry at the displacement and disruption in lives and livelihoods that the bauxite companies have produced all over this country, in communities that haven't been as lucky as these. How I would have mourned the slaughter of the soil in Coffee Grove, where the yearning to grow things and see things grow first took root in me; a district where the longing for land inhabits people like a living thing. I would have mourned for Damion and the loss of his livelihood. I would have mourned for

Congolin, for the loss of his dialogues with the grung. That said, has the threat really disappeared? *What help us now a the sinkhole-dem and the rock stone. Dem no love that,* Damion says; *the mining people no too much inna dem type o' land-de.* It's the rockiness of this land that has saved it from the bauxite companies, he believes, because *dem machine woulda mash up.* Once more, the inherent ruggedness of this terrain emerges, it seems, as a guardian of communal belonging.

In his book *Fugitive, Where Are You Running?,* Dénètem Touam Bona writes that the borders of the Maroon territories 'could only be maintained in their own erasure'. Meaning, simply, that it's the fact of being undesired that protects them. Likewise, I feel, a place such as Mount Pleasant can only be maintained in the untameableness of its land, only by how this land continues to jam the radars of the system that threatens it.

I'm paying attention to what Damion tells me. Yet the Post Office remains lodged like a physical presence inside my ribs. Why do I want to spend time with it, as one spends time with a long-lost, treasured soul? Why do I want to atomise it, examining the parcel scale's every rust flake, every curve and bulge of the posts supporting the weather-worn, stubbornly enduring zinc awning, the joints where wood and ancient mud meet and fuse? The answer seems so obvious. The Post Office helped make me. Don't we often want to re-encounter our origins to see whether we can detect within them any clue about what we were to become? If this is like deciphering an oracle, then how would I know what it was showing me about my life to come? At the same time, what also keeps me wanting to speak to this small wooden structure is the desire to preserve it somehow, to quell my anxiety that it won't always be here – because if it is here, there's something about myself that I can come back to find. If it is here and can keep on being here, I tell myself, then I can have a heritage, a starting point for my story – I can trace my origin to some ground. It's that search for monuments, for signs, for material traces of a history, that lingers in my thoughts.

It's a theme that Derek Walcott, one of the Caribbean's most admired poets, returns to in his work – the desire for a sense of accumulation of ourselves and our past in the land. How can we, descendants of Africans, naked of their original lands, cultures and religions, and remaining naked through the systemic denudation of colonialism, see ourselves as deeply planted in the land? It's through being able to see traces of ourselves and our ancestors in that land. It's through signs of memorialisation. Europeans have all sorts of marble structures, columns, statues, monuments, temples to the glory of their history. We have so little of that – where would we get it in our less than seventy years of self-determination in a violent, cruel and yet beautiful place long dominated by slavery? Our glory, we tell ourselves and the world, is our beaches, coconut trees shading hammocks and blue seas bringing tourists to these shores. That's self-delusion, and anyway, all of that is owned by the rich, the very descendants of the colonists themselves, and wealthy foreigners, mostly white. Again, those places are not like this land, which the colonists don't want.

So, in history, too often my kind of people can't keep things. We're unable to accumulate wealth – we're too precarious, always moving. How much and how often have I moved in my attempt to create wealth? Literally, slavery and colonialism have robbed us of our ability to build: it's all about land, in the end. History is land. So that's the wealth; I've spent decades looking for it in the wrong places. And perhaps, I also tell myself, treasuring this wooden edifice is part of my way of locating myself in *this* earth. Perhaps it's part of my way of building; I can build a sense of myself on this, a mythology of myself on this monument, and that makes me proud. But if it had been razed to the ground, then how would I build that mythology of myself? As with many thoughts I have difficulty articulating, I placed this one in poetry:

> He returned to the little post office in Mount Pleasant for the first time since his childhood – a little comical edifice big with his memories. He was only nine days old when Mama took him under her arm and traversed two villages to arrive at her place of work, first tabernacle of his early childhood. The edifice now engulfed in mad, succulent weeds, it was as though his birth had been covered in rich vegetation, as though it had got smaller, too, as much as time and his travels had been long. All his childhood in this wooden small-ness. How long will you stay there, he thought, before you enter into the earth? And then, what will be left of my birth?

Smallness. This is why I migrated, going to England, France and back again to England. Smallness had given rise to my theory of control, namely, that I could cancel my shame through culture; that I'd have one up on the people who thought they were better than me. I've spent so much of my life trying to emerge from smallness, to conquer it, and in so doing, I've spent much time trying to leave this place. But now look at me coming back. I look at myself as if looking at another person. Re-evaluating my theory of control is about more than the simple question of coming back to Coffee Grove to live – who knows, one day I may be forced to. The point for me is how impossible it is to see the issues in black and white as I did back then, when my life's ambition was to climb the social ladder. Back when Coffee Grove was the dirt, the bush, the place that was keeping us down. The point is how I now see the ingenuity of our lives. The way we lived within smallness without being poor. The way we beautified our roughness. The way we created dignity for ourselves despite our terribleness. But above all, what it's taken me this long to see: our *actual* richness, the security of our food, its wholesomeness, the pride of owning the land – the pride of stepping on it with all the affirmation of belonging, of being at home in it. The way we step out of our houses and are with the earth; the way the land is in us. I've learned to see our roughness and our beauty as intertwined.

Yes, the little Post Office is still there. There are countless wasp nests under the zinc roof, the yard is overgrown with weeds and parts of the stone wall have broken down – but this is the Post Office all right. I walk through the narrow stone opening. There must have been steps there that have now weathered away. My eyes survey the ubiquitous white limestone.

Take some photos. Remember yourself now, here.

A place for what remains
without place: the intimate
histories of minor characters –

intimacies in the ground.
Ground – the sanctuary
where the departed continue to touch
upon our senses.

7.

Gathering the Dispersed

Sta Celona!

It's the fifteenth day of my journey, and as the morning sun bathes Coffee Grove in its glow, I find myself strolling towards the gate of an old woman who holds fragments of my childhood memories. Our paths have rarely crossed in my years of wandering.

There she stands, a silhouette against the rising light.

Come in nuh, a who dat? Mi eye them no good . . . Her voice crackles with age as she peers through fading eyesight. *Then come through the gate nuh?*

Hello, Sta Cel, I greet her, stepping through the gate. *How you do, ma'am?*

On the veranda, Miss Netty, a companion of hers, squints in my direction, her brows furrowed in uncertainty. *A who dis, Sta Cel? You recognise him?* she queries, brows drawn low and tight.

Same Sister Celona, Sta Cel, one of Mama's closest 'brethren' in Coffee Grove, her friend and the holder, probably, of secrets; secrets not quite buried as long as Sta Cel remains alive.

Short body, brown, earthy clay skin. I can see the ghost of her powerful legs in the weak ones I look at now. Sinews keep a memory of how a person used to be. She's old now, her diminished eyesight and the effortfulness of her gait a testimony to this.

No sa, mi can't figure out is who, Sta Cel mutters as she comes closer, head leaning forward and eyes squinting above this cloud of memory, *the voice familiar, but ah can't place the face.* As she inches closer, a flicker of recognition dances across her features, and with a sudden burst of clarity, she points to a chair, inviting me to sit. *Mi glad fi see you, you fat and you brown.* This, for her, is a compliment. *Fat and brown,* she repeats. In these rural districts, 'fat' not only signifies physical robustness, it's shorthand for financial well-being. It's sort of the best compliment that someone can give you when you come back *from foreign.* The *brown,* I imagine, has been thrown in for good measure. 'Brown' denotes a certain lightness of skin tone, an aspiration deeply ingrained within the consciousness of many. These beliefs are testament to a bygone era, shaped by the shadow of the Union Jack. Sta Cel must be in her eighties now.

She hobbles towards the doorway, her movements slow and deliberate, her hand reaching instinctively for something that's no longer there. Empty-handed, she pauses. Before I can gather my thoughts, my curiosity gets the better of me and I enquire about her leg.

What's the trouble? Arthritis? I blurt out. The makeshift bed she'd been sitting on – a mishmash of wooden chairs and cushions – suddenly transforms her in my eyes. I'm reminded of the passage of time, of how those once sturdy calves carried her effortlessly over Coffee Grove's hills to neighbouring villages, where she'd spend hours inside a church, fervently speaking in tongues as she pounded the terrazzo tiles.

No sa, she responds, turning to Miss Netty, who sits nearby. It's like a confidence, as if what Sta Cel's about to say fits into a long, ongoing series of confidences. *A trick them trick it.* With a solemn air, Sta Celona recounts the incident that led to her limp.

One day, she begins, her voice tinged with gravity, *I was coming out the kitchen when I felt somebody shove me. I fall flat on my stomach and I feel a tremor running through my right leg.* She touches the leg tenderly, as if reliving the sensation. *There was no bruise, no blood. Just a turrble heat from the impact.*

Though I'm certain the 'somebody' she refers to isn't of this world, I can't help but interject.

A spirit? I venture.

Sta Cel nods solemnly. *A spirit,* she confirms, her gaze piercing. And in that moment, I glimpse the weight of her conviction.

A hint of the other-worldly to kick-start my day. 'Supernatural' doesn't quite capture the essence of life here, where spirits are woven into the very fabric of existence. It feels like the natural order of things. I sense I'm not yet finished exploring these encounters. In this place, the connection between people and the spirit world is deeply rooted. Mama's dealings with the duppies that occasionally visited our abode were straightforward: *Come outta mi house, mi and you na'ah sleep in ya tonight!* Yet there were times when she'd let them be. Sometimes in the middle of a daytime conversation, she'd recount seeing someone in the house the night before. Once, I remember, it was a woman in a pink lace dress and wide-brimmed hat, peering over the wooden partition between our rooms. *And when the woman eye-dem meet mine, she slowly bend her head back down,* she'd added in tones of intrigue. Her descriptions were vivid, her gestures bringing the scene to life. I'd be filled with dread in these situations, terrified that there was an additional person in the house that I could not see. There were dead people whose presence she welcomed. To see between worlds was a cherished gift.

After what seems like half an hour, I take leave of Sta Cel and Miss Netty. *I'm stretching my legs*, I announce, as a way of saying goodbye to them. *Mi de bout ya fi a likkle while enuh*, I say, so they know they'll be seeing me around. *Round by Miss Rita.*

Tommy is back – a notion that brings smiles all round.

I want to keep walking up the Coffee Grove main road; my destination: Mama's old house. I've nothing but a desire for recollection, for re-experiencing the road. Perhaps I'll re-evoke old sensations. It's a short distance, in fact, to get to Mama's, a length of road I walked countless times by her side, one littered with the homes of many of her brethren.

Back out on the Coffee Grove road, healthy-looking Spanish needle and Guinea grass encroach onto the edges of the rough asphalt, and the leaf of life reaches out to touch the feet of the passer-by. Here, the ground feels close to the body. Space is smaller than in Leeds, tighter, yet the air is fuller. One can smell the humidity of the soil beneath the cabbages, turnips and yam hills lying on either side of the road, along with the fruit trees – mango, plum, guinep, avocado, plantain – and logwood dotted along the grazing pastures that stretch to meet thick woodland. There is no border between these cultivation beds and the edge of the road, as if there were no boundary between the land and its produce and the people who walk alongside it; in this way, the land seems to enter your body. There are occasional walls designating property; these tend to be the boundaries of a dwelling, but there are many acres, sometimes large swathes of unoccupied land, that are communally used for

animal pasture, for gathering wood for cooking and building. The commons.

I was surprised, recently, in my study in Leeds, to encounter the word in the work of E. P. Thompson, that famous
historian of the British working class. All along, I had thought
it was only a Jamaicanism. Now I was discovering that the
very word 'commoner' was a term that originally meant
'people of the common'. Of course, *common* here in rural
Jamaica doesn't mean that everything belongs to everyone.
It's not quite the same as the English idea of *the commons* that
existed prior to 1723, say, and the passage of the Black Act. To
begin with, there's no hunting here, at least not any more.
The Maroons hunted wild pigs in the eastern mountains of
the country, the origin of what we call *jerk pork*, but this part
of the island no longer has the kind of wildlife that would
allow for hunting. And besides, people don't generally grow
crops in the common; they do this on their individual plots,
however small these are. Yet, in the common there are fruit
trees. In fact, it recently dawned on me that the little sweet
mangoes we call *common mango* might be so called because
their tree is the one you find most often dotted throughout
the commons. In the summer, when the mangoes are ripe,
you could practically live off them.

Still, today, to learn of the disappearance of the commons
from the British landscape, a gradual dispossession that
began in the early thirteenth century and reached its violent
apogee with the Black Act of the eighteenth, is enlightening.
Until you grasp the phenomenon of how the commons van-
ished from the English landscape, and the violence that
accompanied this, you can't fully understand how society
came to embrace the concept of private property, taken so
much for granted today. Nor can you fully appreciate how

the nation state consolidated itself around the idea of private property. In the introduction to his seminal book *Whigs and Hunters*, E. P. Thompson pens the following concise, and yet expansive, sentence: 'The British state, all eighteenth-century legislators agreed, existed to preserve the property and, incidentally, the lives and liberties of the propertied.'

With the Acts of Enclosure, land that 'had previously belonged generally to everybody and exclusively to nobody', to use the words of Nick Hayes, began to be privatised by lords and barons. As I researched colonialism and land ownership in Britain, the book *Green Unpleasant Land* by Corinne Fowler, the British literary critic and historian, revealed to me that if the phenomenon of enclosure was accelerated in the eighteenth century, it was in large part as a result of British colonialism, as colonialists used the enormous wealth generated from the enterprise to acquire and enclose large swathes of land in the English countryside. The results of this phenomenon are very visible today in the landscape of rural Britain and in how precious little land is in the hands of the popular classes. To put it quite simply, very few English people have land rights; it's not something protected or enabled by the laws, and that's a fairly direct result of colonial exploitation on the other side of the world.

In Jamaica, not only have we inherited the English word *common* and its concept, but the practices that the term denotes remain alive to a significant extent, even if they have been eroded by the society's progressive turn to globalisation, one that has accelerated since my childhood.

On these peasant mountain roads, the silver glint of sunshine on the beds of cabbages and turnips feels like something I had longed for in my body. The feeling of earthed-ness is intensely *me*, though I've been away for many years. One never leaves. And that silence, generous and full: there's so much happening in it. In Coffee Grove, conversations take up their space in the silence; living in this space involves hearing the language of things, making room for them in your body. Silence is revered here, embraced without fear. To cherish silence is to acknowledge the power of the woodlands and the earth. And when machines make noise – the chainsaw operating in the bush or the distant rumble of a van's engine – they enable you to hear and feel the land in a new way, by disrupting the air. Here, there are winds that whisper ancient voices.

I have often yearned for the same connection in the woodlands in Leeds. Picture this: it's an autumn evening and I'm dressed in my long, black down coat, complete with cowl, and the rest of my clothes are also black or near black, except for my yellow hat. I imagine that I must cut quite a figure as dusk settles on the wood, my five feet and eleven inches elevated by a full yard on the stump of a three-hundred-year-old oak right beside the pathway, and I sense the movement of the last joggers and walkers who pass this way. Dressed in such a way and standing atop what resembles a plinth, my body is in an unusual situation. I did not plan the situation, which I assume might, from a certain point of view, look like something of a performance. I insist on standing on this plinth. It will not be a problem to me.

It's the stump of a tree that I have long admired in the Roundhay Wood, near to where I live. The tree was recently felled to eliminate the hazard it posed to passers-by: it had been rotting for many years and was likely to fall soon. But I want to stand on this broad stump. 'Stump' is such a paltry

word, given what it is, and what it evokes – the vastness of a
continent. I go up on it because I want to think about what
changes for me, about what changes in my busy, email-filled,
technology-driven life, when I stand on this broad stump,
pausing, *just* standing, for a while. Below me, the stump also
evokes a sea, and I feel an immersion in something broader
than myself.

I do not know what I get from standing on this former
tree, which still is and will continue to be a tree, but something changes. I become more conscious of my body, of its
fluidity and evanescence. I become more conscious of the
tree and of the ways it connects to me. The wood beneath
my feet is muscular, solid, unmoving, though I can't help
but think of all the movements of food and nutrients that
have accreted over hundreds of years to produce this live
expanse of wood that I call 'a stump of a tree'. It's a different
rhythm I feel to when I am just walking on the black soil of
the track. I stand here also to remember what it feels like to
simply stand on the stump of a tree. Doing so slows down
my perception of the movement of time and of my body's
movement in time. It reminds me that I am more than my
job by reminding me of childhood times in which this,
standing on a tree stump, was something significant, something worth all my attention.

But standing here creates problems. It is 4.45 p.m. on
18 November and now there is very little light remaining by
which one can see other bodies. My dark body that insists on
being here creates problems for other people. I insist that it
won't create problems for me. Two teenage cyclists ride by
and one shouts over his shoulder, 'You can't stand up there,
buddy.' This encapsulates the dilemma of entrepreneurial
walking, or the idea of walking as a leisure activity within

the framework of productivity culture: you can't stand – stopping is disruptive.

Though many years have passed since my last visit, I envision Mama's house, nestled amidst the twists and turns of the road. I ascend the hill from where Sta Cel resides at its base. Following the road's curve, I come, on the left, to Mammy Scille's house, where I spent much time playing, romping in the fields with her numerous grandchildren. On the right, the church and its yard, another focal point of my early years. Beyond the church, another ascent awaits, a small hill leading to Mama's house. The long-abandoned edifice is currently being refurbished by my mother. Mommy happens to be there today, working. I'm eager also to see the land and to feel it, meaning, to feel the embodiment of all that I have missed about this place by being away, of all that has missed *me* as the place goes on living in my absence. I'm curious to see the state of the land in which I plan to inter, in a few days' time, the navel strings of my two daughters. In our traditions, these, too, are planted, and I relish the idea of planting parts of my daughters' bodies in the land on which I grew up, nourishing the hope, as our ancestors always have, that I'll be planting my children here. I walk slowly, and the earth rushes into me from both sides of the road.

The land is as rocky as it's always been and is currently relatively bare; it's recently been cleared of the growth of bushes and shrubbery that had overtaken it since Mama's death, returning this home, as they say, to the brutal wildness of nature. One of the most striking sights that greets me as I gaze upon the landscape is the coconut tree beneath which my own umbilical cord is buried. Over time – since I first observed it properly, notably after Mama's passing in 2012 – it has taken on an unusual form, bending sharply at a right angle so that roughly eight metres of its trunk now stretches horizontally, parallel to the ground. I think the tree might have been broken once – in a storm? – where it now bends. I've come to see this tree as an extension of my person. Perhaps the angle of the tree means absolutely nothing, but then again . . . The animist in me still finds reassurance in its enduring presence.

The house's roof is off, and I can just about see the cerulean blue of a tarpaulin, presumably covering whatever valuables remain inside; this includes Mama's lacquered Formica dresser, which I want to see again – her *England chest*, as I used to think of it, since it bears an English address, that of its sender. I later discovered that Mama had no connection to this former owner. Nevertheless, the chest remained a permanent fixture in the house, storing some of her cherished possessions.

There's been speculation that her hopes and dreams find continuity within me. If nothing else, it's a comforting thought. It does seem reasonable to think that Mama is hanging around here, if we accept that her cells have interacted with and irrevocably entered this place, in these rocks on which she hung her blue-soap-treated white clothes to dry; this veranda on which she spent time, chatting with passing people as they called out to her; these windows through which she transacted her petty commerce of seasoning salt and black pepper, of fee-fee (whistle-like toys) and balloons for children, of batteries for radios and lamps. Perhaps that *too* is what our people mean by *duppy*, the unmistakable sense of a trace of the stories, of the images that remain, traces that seem to produce, to the point of being inseparable from it, a sense of the body. If so, there are duppies all around and I see them all the time.

On the hushed veranda of the house, a puddle of rainwater glistens, casting reflections of the dim afternoon light. The air is heavy with the scent of moist resin. Outside, the marl heap, recently disturbed, reveals its fresh, earthy core beneath a layer of moss. Adjacent to it, a stack of boards sits atop the veranda, awaiting purpose.

This yard is another place of *recueillement* that deserves its time. As I reach the backyard, Mommy is there, on the stony hillside behind the house. She's lighting a fire inside a duck ants' heap. *To kill them before they make their way into the house*, she says. My attention is drawn to the stones, here again. These are the ones on which Mama used to spread out clothes for the sun's action to loosen stubborn dirt stains. On these, I climbed up to meet Sanjie, the granddaughter of our neighbour, Brother B, and admire her round face and ebony-coloured skin. On these, I tried to hop and jump while playing by myself, before realising how sharp they were, how I would get scratches and cuts on my legs. Under these stones, galliwasps lived and they would slither out to inflict on the unsuspecting person a venomous sting; so it was thought – *beware, do not stay too close to them*, Mama would warn. She never tried to have these rocks removed. Perhaps she didn't find them to be an issue, or to be unaesthetic. Perhaps the cost of dislodging them, which might mean dumping mined topsoil on the ground and levelling it off with a large amount of mortar, was too prohibitive. Perhaps she found it natural to live with them.

Mama lived with this rocky ground, which she tamed, charmed, as she charmed everything, making it work. There was never any curated garden here; Mama was not that kind of gardener. Her passion was for plants in the wild. Though she did insist on beautifying her surroundings: she would decorate and embellish her home with doilies and figurines, with motifs painted onto the walls of the house or designed in roughcast, but above all, by buffing floors and wooden furniture, making surfaces gleam. Yes, she would gather blooming flowers and plants into a bouquet that she'd place in a vase sitting on the dinner table, and the front yard, like any front yard in any village in Jamaica, was lined with a hedge of colourful plants, sown there once and for all and growing naturally in the fertile soil, the flowers appreciated for their appearance in their season: allamandas, crotons and poinsettias – things that needed little or no mainten-ance, for Mama's free time was spent in the grung.

It was there that Mama invested her energy. I suppose necessity also took her there, but it seems to me now that she thrived in that environment. It was also during those trips to and from the grung that she'd walk slowly and inten-tionally, foraging for wild herbs, for medicine. They were for use, of course, but where's the line between usefulness and pleasure in these matters? There was no curated garden in the yard, no intentional potting of plants, no daily tending and setting, no regular monitoring of growth, as in my mother's improvised veranda garden in Mandeville.

Instead, in Mama's garden, there were plants for wellness, herbs that grew wild: peppermint, with its lance-like leaves that were regularly picked for their heady benediction in the morning; vervain, for its soothing of stomachs and its calm-ing effect, promoting good sleep, and for the wild blue blessing of its candelabra-like spikes; strong back, with its musky base notes, Mama using the tiny green petals of this spreading creeper shrub to treat back pain. The backyard needed only a little weeding to keep these wildflowers growing and to prevent the undesired herbs from taking over. Among the herbs left to grow wild to heal us, there were occasional food trees and vines, chocho, avocado, coconut, and the odd bed of tomatoes. Besides, things often sprang up in the wild backyard from seeds simply thrown out there – *dash-out*, we say – as kitchen refuse. From this you might get an unexpected harvest of pumpkins from a vine you didn't even suspect was running there, underneath the avocado tree. Likewise, the thriving ackee tree now growing out of the stone wall that bounds the land on the street side simply sprang up from a seed that Mama *dashed* out there. Such is the particular charm of Mama's backyard, nothing different from how most families use their land here. And as children, these wild backyards and backlands were where we played.

Amidst these musings, I find myself wondering: Was this backyard always so small? Was the wall always so low? Do individuals raised in large settings – farms, mansions, palaces – perceive them as smaller upon returning after years elsewhere? The elsewhere places I've resided in, from France to Britain to Canada, boast vastness, but I'm not just thinking about the scale of countries. It's not just that, scale-wise, Jamaica's landscapes, however sublime, are modest in comparison to the other countries I've lived in. It's also that the spaces of my childhood truly were small. I didn't know that all along, but now I understand it.

Considering the inside of the house and how diminutive it now appears to me, I can't help but think that Mama enlarged her small spaces through the way she lived in them, the way she made them her own, which simply entailed staking her right to them, her right to have a place of her own. That assertion of space, crafted through sheer determination, that's how I interpret this transformation of the minuscule into the undeniably beautiful – expansive in its own essence. This is what she accomplished when, defying obstacles, she took her child and left her husband's abode, subsequently embarking on the gradual construction of this hillside dwelling, all while leasing a back room in the home of a fellow church member. And once she got here, she inhabited this house proudly.

A part of what's fascinating about this smallness is how it was never actually small. There's a beauty in that, a creation of 'possibility in the space of enclosure', as Saidiya Hartman would put it, a startling *method of beauty*. It's in my eyes that this house is transfigured. For a few months now, Mommy has been on a mission to tame the unruly mass of weeds and overgrown shrubbery of the backyard into some sort of a garden. She's planted her flowers, both potted and non-potted, but, different to Mama's backyard, this backyard garden of hers will contain far more cultivation. For cultivation, Mama had her grung, leased to her by the Powells. What ambition for this rather tiny space! Again, what I'd always considered as tiny. It reminds me of Congolin's rocky hillside, charmed into a verdant kingdom.

And speaking of Congolin, he's the one who's been helping Mommy clear the land, getting rid of persistent weeds by using old methods instead of herbicides, including fire and, well, plain old weeding. Incredible to see him work and make light sport of this impressive tangle. He approaches the hard labour with good humour and incredible generosity – the old community solidarity. He's meticulous, though, and so his slashing, burning and chopping takes a few weeks as he alternates between this and the tasks of his own farm. He has to make several trips down from the hills where he works.

As the land is cleared, Mommy begins the planting: a royal palm for beautification in the middle of the sloping backyard – Mommy will always be Mommy, thinking of beautification first; a Parson Brown orange tree, under which we'll bury the navel string of our secondborn, Agni; and a June plum tree, where the cord of our firstborn, Leyla, will be interred. *I hope they will be bearing fruit the next time they come to Jamaica,* my mother says. Also, lemon, Otaheite apple, pomegranate, Julie mango, custard apple, soursop (underneath which my niece Skylar's navel string is planted – *everybody has their tree,* says Mommy), breadfruit, papaya, pumpkin running all 'bout the place, arrowroot, corn, Gungo peas, three scallion plants, thyme, rosemary, string beans, cassava, aloe vera, an almond tree – *I've planted this so I can have shade,* she says, and looking out over her handiwork, she beams with pride. The cicadas suddenly raise a din. It's only a quarter past ten in the morning and already I've seen so much! Mommy has just set fire to the stump of a cedar tree that had rotted and therefore been chopped down to make space for more cultivation. In sum, her mission is to transform this little backyard space, less than a square of land, into a proper farm to feed herself and be well in her body.

I take pleasure in seeing her work, cleaning up the land and getting it ready for cultivation. I find joy in observing her own enjoyment in doing this. It's *her* land now. I also spend time walking around inside the little house, my first home, taking photos of objects – intact objects and ones that have fallen apart because of mildew and rain; things that are still whole and stuff that's rotting; an old yard shoe; a brush; a clothes basket; chipboard dining-room chairs; curtains still hanging on a curtain rod; the old barrel inside which Mommy has placed nearly all the books I've left in her home over the years. I will want to remember what things look like, and these photos will help me, but they do more than help one remember. There's something physical about them. Together, they're the closest thing to a memorial. To paraphrase the philosopher Jean-Luc Nancy, I gather objects to write, I write to touch the body.

I spend the balance of the morning and the early afternoon with Mommy, pitching in with the clearing up of cut grass and shrubbery and the dislodging of burnt stumps. By two thirty, I'm ready to head down the hill to meet Norrel, a farmer friend. We've planned to visit his farm together, and I'm looking forward to seeing it first-hand.

As I arrive at his home, he's leading his goats *out to bush* with machete in hand, as all the farmers do. We walk just over a hundred metres to reach the pasture, one of the many plots he tends to. Amidst patches of turnips, carrots and potatoes, there's a swathe of bush where his goats roam freely. Norrel belongs to the esteemed Martins, one of the long-standing landowning families of Coffee Grove whose roots trace back three generations in this district, presumably to the late nineteenth century. Mama would sometimes lament the fact that she had only *one likkle piece o' rockstone*, while these people held such large amounts of property. Those who had land were, in my eyes, always enveloped in a kind of mystique. I looked yearningly at the way they walked distances to get to their bush, or grung; at how they could walk distances on land they themselves owned. I marvelled at their bushes, woodlands, barely penetrable spaces that one could get lost in. I envied the farmers returning from pasture with their scarlet-soiled water boots and machetes. I would consider, with a tribal envy, the trips with animals in hand, small ones such as goat kids, large ones such as donkeys, and even larger ones – cattle.

I express my admiration to Norrel. *Who you say sell you da piece a land-ya again?* I enquire, my mind still lingering on the histories of land transactions in the area, on the intricacies I long to know.

Mr Peddy. See him house ova yasso, he replies, with a gesture across the pasture.

As a child, the mere mention of Mr Peddy's name carried weight, signalling affluence and status. His years spent in England endowed him with an aura of prestige upon his return to Coffee Grove, when he joined the ranks of revered 'returning residents' whose wealth and stature preceded them.

Mr Peddy, and others like him, possessed large expanses of land that, at the time, beggared my imagination. I was intimidated by such folk, including Norrel, still in his youth back then. Their presence commanded respect, their wealth measured not so much in money terms but in the sheer expanse of their holdings. In fact, Mr Peddy, despite his vast holding, had probably worked menial jobs in England, like most of the other peasants who migrated to that country in the wake of the Second World War. But they worked hard, and the modest incomes they earned translated into considerable wealth upon their return. That said, long before mass migration to Britain, families like the Peddys and the Martins had amassed considerable holdings. I wonder now about the endeavours that paved the way for this.

What legacy lay behind the abundance of land they possessed? Small quantities when compared to the plantations, certainly, but considerable on the scale of the peasantry. How did certain families, like the Peddys and the Martins, ascend to become prominent landowners while others, like my own grandmother, remained on the periphery?

Though I can now envisage owning a bit of land myself, I still experience land ownership by people who are from my background as a sort of magic exerting a spell on my imagination. Likewise, I experience the exclusion from land as a form of bewitchment, if not a curse. Standing alongside Norrel, gazing at the diminished grandeur of Mr Peddy's home, the aura of power surrounding it nevertheless remains present, despite the passage of time, casting a shadow of intimidation I've yet to outgrow.

Even now, I find myself instinctively deferring to the perceived stature of the big man. Back in the day, I wouldn't dare go knock on his gate. It's certainly the mystique that remains, since now I have financial resources at my disposal. That said, I still do not have land. Tribal envy.

And yet here, in the district, and in much of rural Jamaica, land isn't seen as a commodity for profit as much as a holding, to be just that – *held*, passed down from generation to generation. The idea of land as a powerful link, connecting the living community to their ancestors, is observed in the practice, still alive in this and similar parts of Jamaica, of burying your dead on your land. The dead remain with the living; they are, indeed, part of the affective value of the land, something that might seem strange to those who do not understand the kind of social structure in which ancestrality plays an active role.

In capitalism, people need to buy a space for their death. Land is too valuable, too precious to accommodate our human remains. So land must be rationalised. In the rich countries of the North, good land is devalued if one buries people on it. You have cemeteries in which to stock the dead, sometimes on top of each other. In tiny spaces. Often, you rent these spaces for a certain number of decades. At the Père-Lachaise Cemetery in Paris, for instance, a standard gravesite lease is for thirty years. Then you have to make way for another dead someone. It's just business.

I realise, musing about this, how radically differently we think of our land here. There are different ideas about its meaning. There are visible graves on people's property; it's natural. The dead are a part of family; they need to be near, must be present in conversations. Why would you think of placing them far away from you? There's no talk of the devaluation of property here because that land is never going to be sold; it was never *meant* to be sold. Why would one sell the land of one's ancestors? The land is a community of the living and the dead. Here, the dead are comfortable, with nobody trying to dislodge them, nobody giving them a set time or trying to rob them of their space. They have more than ample room and are at ease.

Contemplating the sight of tombs just lying within yards, you realise how naturally they integrate into the landscape. How they punctuate the scenery, positioned in different parts of the dwelling space, depending on the size or shape of the land. Their placement varies – just beside the house, situated in the front yard, or nestled deeper into a spacious garden. In larger yards, family cemeteries may lie near the roadside, with the house further inland, accessible via a dirt track. It's the family alone who decide – no planning permission needed. No parish council permission for how to bury your dead.

The bauxite earth hardens to smooth, slick surfaces that become treacherous after rain, as they are this afternoon when Norrel and I begin our ascent up the hill. We're headed towards his main grung – the field we've just been in is mainly grazing pasture for his goats. In my mind, the grung we're going to is not a mappable place, except in the way it's mapped by the bodies traversing these terrains. The land defies marking, resists the outsider's eye.

Once we've passed the houses at the bottom of the hill, there's not a soul in sight. As I follow Norrel, I've seen more Jamaica Hope and Brahman cows than humans. The dogs you find darting around you in any wood in England are absent here. What's more present is the protective voice of the woodland, which may seem solitary, though it is not unpeopled. You see sections that have been cleared in anticipation of a planting, clearings in which a cow lies tied to a stake in the ground, areas of tillage, a fenced-off field at the edge of a thick, forested growth, fruit trees – jackfruit, limes, bananas, star apple – on either side of the path. In this rainforest, human presence mingles seamlessly with animal and plant life. It's a coexistence.

The absence of the term 'forest' in our vernacular speaks volumes; it reflects our intimate relationship with this environment. As a child, I yearned for the forests depicted in fairy tales, only to realise that our native landscapes held a different kind of magic, one that Western narratives often overlook. It hit me that this woodland is not an *outside place* – that is the etymological meaning of *forest*, from the Latin *foris*, meaning 'outside' – but one that is within. Life takes place within the bush, the rainforest; there's a whole economy here – there are farms, there are food trees, there are animals. An ecosystem and an economy – some might call it 'marginal', 'informal', but our inability to see this kind of living as an economy in its own right raises questions about our view of the world.

A suppleness comes alive in Norrel's body as he moves glidingly over the rocks, his feet finding their place amongst jutting boulders. Here, I realise, there's no smooth kind of walking, none of the sort you can do without looking down. Looking down might not actually be *looking down*. You learn the space, you take the space into your body, so that your muscles, your feet and legs become familiar with it. Is it a choreography? Your body always becomes familiar with your space, embraces it. Nevertheless, the land of rocks is a shock.

Standing on Norrel's six-acre piece of land in the hills – it's taken us just under an hour of walking to get here – I see all sorts of fruit trees, avocado, soursop, Otaheite apple, mango, scattered across the land, interspersed among plots of yams. He identifies the different varieties, bringing back to memory things no longer familiar – Sinvinsen, round-leaf yellow yam, negro yam – and spices: pimento, bissy . . . Yet it's the Sinvinsen yam vine that captivates me most, streaked with vibrant hues where stem meets stalk and at the tendrils.

I've exchanged money for freshly harvested sweet potatoes, their earthy aroma still clinging to the soil. A mere two hundred Jamaican dollars for three pounds – a bargain! And already I'm making plans to return in a few days for yams, eager to delve deeper into Norrel's agricultural bounty.

You feed yourself mostly off your land? I venture, curious about Norrel's dietary habits, and, by extension, whether Coffee Grove traditions endure.

The only thing we go a supermarket for a likkle rice, he answers. I suspect there may be a few other items, but in his own way he tells me all I need to know. His realm is brimming with plenty, a cornucopia of seasonal delights complemented by the livestock – pigs, cattle, poultry – tended by him and his kin, all contributing to a sustainable food economy. The ritual of 'killing days' still thrives as a communal affair where the impending demise of some animal is announced and villagers eagerly await their share of the bounty. You send news around the village that you're about to kill a goat: *Cutie a kill goat this Saturday*, for instance. People prepare their money, knowing where they'll get meat from; and somebody is always *killing*. The prices are a fraction of supermarket rates.

As Norrel elaborates, I gain insight into the intricacies of the local economy. The proceeds from his pimento, yam and other harvests provide the means to procure items not cultivated on his land. Though his children are grown, the importance of food diversity remains paramount for him and his partner. In this verdant district, each farming household contributes to a collective larder, where variety thrives and abundance knows no bounds – a testament to the enduring bond between the people and the land they call home.

Lost in the labyrinth of Norrel's landholdings, I struggle to keep pace with the coordinates swirling in my mind. Six acres here, sixteen more to the south and yet another plot down on Jokoto Hill – *A legacy from mi granny*, he says – but the pride exuding from his voice as he recounts his cultivation exploits is tremendous. He regales me with tales of seizing deals when land was plentiful and cheap – a stark contrast to the present, where deep pockets are a requisite for acquisition. His recent partnership with his son to purchase a new parcel, earmarked for goat tethering, speaks volumes about his vision for the future. Although he has mainly financed the venture, he envisions a day when the land will pass into his son's hands.

As we mount further into the hills, Norrel gestures towards swathes of land, sharing stories of families and their generational ties to the soil. The narrative of children inheriting or taking over the land is imbued with profound significance for him, a sentiment I come to share. To Norrel, continuity is paramount – what matters is to have continuity, for young people today to be interested in the type of life that he and so many others live in Coffee Grove. *They might not come up here to wuk grung*, he reflects, *but at least they have it to sell back and make money, if they want.*

His musings on the intrinsic value of land strike a chord within me. *Yu cyaan go wrong wid lan'*, he declares, *cah dem nah mek no mo' a it.* In a world where assets can be mass-produced, land stands as an immutable bulwark against uncertainty – a safeguard for future generations. I'm drawn to thoughts of Mama's land, her legacy now undergoing a resurrection as my mother embarks on its renovation. After years of estrangement, she's poised to return, finding solace and belonging in the very soil Mama once tended. As I ponder the cyclical nature of life, I can almost hear Mama's exclamatory old African laughter echoing from her grave.

Beauty hides behind the scenes of the sublime. To find it, we will demolish

that scenery.

8.

Miss Ivey's Garden

After the long drive from Coffee Grove to Portland, traversing the North Coast Highway and St Mary's verdant vistas, I find myself on the uphill path to the Moore Town Maroon settlement. Pulling over at a roadside shop, I enquire about Madda. With a calm gesture of the hand, a young man, leaning down to my car window, directs me to a sturdy figure nearby. This is the individual with whom I'm to speak. The stout man, with an air of taciturn authority, looks at me with an assessing gaze. It's clear he's the gatekeeper to the enigmatic herbalist.

A recent conversation with Marsha, a friend from Kingston, stirred intrigue as she regaled me with a tale of this mysterious woman from Portland. *She's well known in the area, and people come from all over to see her for her knowledge of bush medicine*, Marsha said, telling me about the curative bath Madda had prepared for her husband. *It's Ivelyn Harris, but if you go there and ask for Madda, you're bound to find her, 'cause everybody knows her.*

My curiosity piqued, I plunged into online research, convinced that meeting this woman held the promise of invaluable lore and insight. Like Congolin, Madda appears to be another conduit to the plants' secrets, another plant telegrapher.

In a curt manner, the man probes, questioning my motives for seeking out Madda's expertise. Am I here for healing?

His words hint at something beyond my comprehension. But, undeterred, I reveal myself as a Jamaican writer conducting research, explaining my keen interest in Madda's practice.

Nodding wordlessly, the man motions for me to follow, leading the way into the churchyard, where Madda speaks to clients from a window at the rear of the church.

Me can't talk to you now, she says as I approach the window. I read sincerity in her eyes as she apologises for the delay. Already behind schedule, she explains that her morning fatigue has left her with a backlog of eager patients awaiting her attention.

Among them, a young man appears anxious, eager for his turn. Despite my position ahead of him in the queue, Madda discerns the urgency of his needs – his case concerns healing. Meanwhile, I've already informed Madda that my purpose is to discuss medicinal plants and dreams for my research. She acknowledges this with a serene authority that suggests such topics are well within her realm of expertise. She names the gruff man as one of the *securities* who work for her. If I keep speaking to him, she says, indicating the orderly progression of her appointments, I'll know when my turn is near.

In the Mount Olivet AME Zion Church, all sorts of people are waiting – young men in their twenties, middle-aged men and women; local people, people with foreign accents; those with walkers, those with no visible complaints. In the sanctuary of the church, a hen walks around, cackling. Madda's gruff security comes out to ask, *A who next?* The women beside me look around, then at each other, hesitating. Like everybody else in the sanctuary, they're here for healing. The security gets cross: why are the people not lined up, waiting their turn, why must he waste time going outside to look for people? Eventually, three people come into the building and take their seat on the bench next to the door that leads to Madda's healing room. They're happy and talkative, speaking with American accents, their conversation punctuated by occasional laughter. I have no book with me. It would have made the wait so much easier. How will I endure it? I look around at the painted scenes of a white Jesus with his disciples and the Woman at the Well that canvas the church's walls.

An hour and a half goes by like this and it's almost midday. Outside, where the heat is debilitating, I walk labouredly up a slope in search of a phone signal. As I do so, a group of men sharing Guinness catches my eye. Doubt gnaws at me – have I been waiting for the right person? Is she truly the herbalist Marsha directed me to? The doubts linger, mocking the earnestness of my patience under the scorching sun.

One man voices his certainty – this woman is not Ivelyn Harris. *She a no Harris at all.* Is she even a herbalist? The man's doubts deepen my own. Marsha's recommendation had led me to search the internet for Harris's identity and her authored works. But now, faced with conflicting information, I feel I may have wasted the morning.

The man dials a number, but then his attention shifts to a passing woman. *You know a woman round here named Ivelyn Harris?* he asks. She confirms their acquaintance, clarifying that Ivelyn lives further up the mountain, in the village of Cornwall Barracks. Decision made, we agree to head there together. As we drive, she shares local tales and her familial ties to Colonel Harris, a highly respected Maroon colonel who headed the Moore Town settlement for decades. The pieces of the puzzle begin to align. *Is a Rasta woman,* she mentions. *She do healing too, and whole heap of people from Town and from foreign come look fi her.*

We make it to Ivelyn Harris's home. It's a one-mile journey that's taken well over twenty minutes by car because of the state of the roads. The bush specialist introduces herself as *Ivelyn or Blossom, a direct descendant of Nanny of the Maroons.* Ivelyn is a dark-skinned woman with long, neat dreadlocks that fall to her waist. She looks to be in her late sixties. She walks unhurriedly, with an aura of tranquillity and ease that brings the word *fearless* to my mind. I ask whether I can call her Miss Ivey and, with a laugh, she acquiesces to my use of this moniker. At the same time, she says, *Mi no really have no time fi the research today you know; I'm on my way down to my other house, the one down the hill . . .* She needs to *pick something urgently* off some tree or another, *because I don't want the birds to get them,* and *because people are picking them before I get a chance to reap them.* It seems a refrain in my life as a researcher that whenever I get to the home of someone I'd like to speak with, that person is on their way somewhere, does *not really have the time for that kind of conversation today,* etc., etc. Is Ivelyn Harris *studying* me? Isn't this what Maroon healers are supposed to do – study you to see if you're the kind of person they can share their knowledge with, the sort of 'researcher' they could even have a conversation with? *Ah don't really have the time, I'm on my way out . . .* seems a filler, taking up the time needed to ascertain my motives, to see *if mi spirit take him.*

The yard is nestled at the end of a grassy track and the bush and woodlands surrounding it throb densely with life. Ivelyn invites me to sit on the veranda, and I hear the tweeting of birds – the yard is a haven for them – while the noise of the crickets swells, then subsides as suddenly as it arose. On Ivelyn's cool veranda, the wait for Madda in the AME Zion Church now seems like an age ago. Madda's church also feels like a different planet. Nevertheless, I resolve to go back to the old healing woman, thinking that she too may have interesting things to share with me. It's an opportunity to learn from the perspective of another type of healer. Besides, it feels wrong to simply drive away without saying anything further to Madda, who'd kindly agreed to speak to me – as if, *Oh, I've found the person I came to look for, and it wasn't you.* For now, though, I'm ecstatic to be on the veranda of Miss Ivey's cottage. *Boy, you favour mi grandson, sa*, she says. That gives me points as well, as I start the tape recorder and begin to introduce myself.

There are other buildings deep down in her yard that are obfuscated by the luxuriant garden of herbs that occupies my view. I spot various green plants, their blossoms catching my eye, many of them triggering a sense of familiarity – from my childhood to the recent weeks spent rediscovering the healing flora of Coffee Grove: country elbow, sarsaparilla, vervain. She introduces me to a whole new set of herbs – I won't remember most of them, but I'm taking notes in my book – many of them different from those Congo uses in his practice.

Some herbs can drink green, others you have to dry. I look out on the lush herb garden separating her dwelling from the cottage where she makes curative baths treating all sorts of ailments (and where clients come to see her from as far as the USA, Canada and the UK). It's only two in the afternoon as she begins to recount to me facts about the herbs in her garden, about how she uses them, about how her ancestors, the Maroons, have used them throughout the centuries. *My herbal knowledge come from the older people in the village, and I get a few dreams as well,* says Miss Ivey. Her interest in plants first came about as a result of accompanying her auntie Liz, the midwife of Cornwall Barracks, on missions. *When Auntie Liz come to deliver the baby,* she begins,

I would follow her to pick the herbs, specific herbs to make a bath for the mother to get back her strength, and to wipe down the baby. I saw the herbs that she pick. She would come back home, put the herbs on the fire, before going inside to deliver the baby.

Quietly excited, I feel, here, that I'm about to enter scarcely known territory. *After she throw out the baby bath,* Miss Ivey continues, *I would go and look at the bush to see how they look when they are boiled, different from when they are fresh.* Miss Ivey penetrates a lost world:

That was when I was about five, and I grow up with that know-ledge. My grandmother Con' Teesha was another notorious herbalist. Anything do that woman, a bush she sen' you go pick, she no go a doctor. So I come up and adopt that principle.

Not seeing Western medicine as the only acceptable kind, or indeed the most authoritative, is nothing foreign to me, since, like Miss Ivey, I grew up with that knowledge. The Maroons have, throughout the centuries, embraced a different healing system to Western pharmaceutical medi-cine. Doing so has been, in some ways, a form of resistance, although it's also, simply, the natural practice of long-held beliefs. The Maroon community is an alternative world, one whose very origin lies in a resistance to the slave plantation and all it symbolised, notably capitalism. I do not reject Western medicine and I acknowledge its contributions, but I also realise that to reject the pharmaceutical industrial complex is also to resist some of the worst aspects of the capitalist paradigm.

When treating patients, Miss Ivey sometimes gets revelations from the spirit world about which plants to use together. As with Congolin, these revelations come in the form of dreams or in a kind of intimation given to her by the plants themselves while she's awake, as if the plants were *calling out to her*. Other times, it's her intuition. But she carries so much knowledge within her, the healing traditions passed down from her Maroon ancestors, that I imagine it might be difficult to characterise exactly what *intuition* is in this case. Is it that so-called inner sixth sense? Or is it a deep-seated knowledge that simply gets activated upon contact with the plants as she walks among them in her garden?

Herbs work slowly, she points out. Cures are not instant; one has to wait for the bushes to exert their effect and stick to a treatment over time – often weeks – believing that things are happening in the background. This is different from the instantaneity or speed I've come to associate with prescriptions I get from the doctor, which are meant to start producing results right away – a mentality I have developed along with most patients in the West. A medicine is effective when we see it *acting* immediately: that's what we mean when we say that the medicine is *working*. But here, Miss Ivelyn introduces a different perspective on time in relation to the medicine she uses and prescribes to her clients. Waiting can be a challenge, but in the Maroon medicine that Miss Ivey practises, the treatment for an ailment is often a revealed one, which immediately places us in a different rhythm of time. *This is not divine healing*, she emphasises, *it's just the knowledge of the plants.* But perhaps when you develop confidence in the ancestors' guidance and the power of the plants, you learn to wait. Waiting, Miss Ivey suggests, is part of a healing system that is holistic, curing hidden sources of the problem rather than just the manifested ailment. She illustrates her point about timescales with a personal anecdote. It's about a case of appendicitis she had when she was eighteen years old.

> *The doctor had me in the hospital for two days with saline water . . . The second night I dreamt my grandmother . . . nothing was wrong with me in the dream. After she call me, I went to the fence where she was standing. She said to me, 'Go home and drink this.' When she said* this*, I noticed that she was standing on a lovely field of Mary Goules. I told the doctor on the third day that I was not going to take the operation, I'm going home.*

Without revealing her reason, she left the hospital under the reproving gaze of the head doctor, who gave her a sweet cup of syrup after making her sign a discharge note. *Come and sign your death warrant*, he said. *As I stood waiting on a taxi outside of the University Hospital*, Ivelyn recounts now, *I felt like if a breeze blew, it would blow me over.* On her way home, meeting a neighbour who also happened to be a farmer, she told him about her situation, asking him whether he knew Mary Goules. Uncannily, this man had been weeding the plant out of his farm in Red Hills and discarding it. The next day, Ivelyn was drinking it. *I start drinking it from it green*, she says, *I drink it two weeks on. Because that's what my grandmother told me – that you mustn't drink no herbs, no medication, longer than two weeks.*

You do it two weeks, then you skip a week, and go back if necessary.

So I drank it two weeks on, one week off; two weeks on, one week off; two weeks on . . . then, you see the next week off, my period came. Then I went to the toilet to pee, and I felt something drop out.

It wasn't a clot. A clot would feel denser; it was something like the size of a penny. It was a veined clump, *a purplish-bluish ball that cut off and drop.* From that day till now, she concludes, she hasn't been sick to the point where she has needed to go to a doctor. It was shortly after this incident that she returned to Cornwall Barracks to live and work with herbs, because *my ancestors' spirit wouldn't leave me alone.*

Miss Ivey is a plain-spoken, uneffusive kind of person, respectful but unornamental in communication – she's definitely the kind of person who *studies* you before letting down her guard. Yet there's an unmistakable tenderness in her voice when she speaks about the flowers in her garden, a tenderness suggesting familiarity and attachment: these are the beings among whom she lives. She takes delight in naming them, inviting me to walk about the herb garden to show me some of the plants she lives with. She names a great many of them and also, like Congolin, she sometimes tests me to see what and how many I know. Mary Goules – not to be confused with marigold. Bachelor button, the curer of cancers. Sarsaparilla. Wild hops, purple vervain. Bitter albott, known in Jamaica as jackass bitters.

With all this conversation around intuition versus dreams in relation to how she uses plants, I want to ask Miss Ivey, and I do, *Do the plants speak to you? Is there a communication process between the herbs and you?*

She laughs, and it's one of the few moments of our conversation where her face visibly lights up with excitement. She doesn't wait for me to finish.

Between me and the herbs? Let me give you this one:

When I tell people, them don't believe me you know . . . One night, when I was 'bout thirty-eight or thirty-nine . . . I used to make traditional Maroon craft and I used to go to Montego Bay to walk up and down and sell . . . and one night when I come to Port Antonio, like eight or nine o'clock when you can't get any vehicle to come home, I walked – had no choice – had to walk to get home.

Incidentally, the distance from Port Antonio to Cornwall Barracks is roughly eleven miles.

So one night I got a drive come to Seeman Valley, she continues, *and same as I come out of the transport, the rain start to fall, so I put my bag on my head and I start to walk. And I walk and I walk and I walk. 'Cause from Seeman Valley to up here is roughly 'bout three and half to four miles. And there was two hibiscus at the gate, one to either side . . . When I was coming up the straight to get to this house, I felt so lonely, because me wet now, tired and everything, so me feel a lonely feeling just come down on me, 'cause me one was living up here . . . As soon as I reach the gate there –* she points to where an iron gate is now erected – *and open it, the two hibiscus just reach out and hug me . . . hug me 'e know! And from that day till today, I never feel lonely again. And when I tell my friends this, they say, 'Ivey, you mussa did smoke some weed.' Hear me, stop talk foolishness! I tell you that I'm walking all the way up, so there was nothing in the space, it was just clear head space, and the two hibiscus reach out and hug me . . . hug me 'e know!* She looks at me as if to say, I know it's hard to believe. *The two of them reach out and hug me, and it was . . . surreal. And I say, oh my God* – she says this looking out into the garden, speaking low, as if reliving the moment, a slight tremor in her voice – *the two herbs them hug me up? Two of them, one on that side and one on the other side . . . and I never feel lonely, from that day until today. No matter where me go by meself.*

It's like that moment give you a level of revelation, I suggest.

Yeah. It give me a satisfaction, it give me a fullness that I had never experienced, you know what I mean . . . And from that, my herbal skill just grow and grow . . . I wrote three books . . .

I have seen them online, I say, and Miss Ivey has copies to show. The book *Healing Herbs of Jamaica*, published by Ian Randle Publishers in Kingston, is one I know will be useful for my research. Continuing without veering off course, I add, *So it looks like in that experience, you get a sense of the liveliness and the communicative power of the plants.*

A spirit! Plants have spirit! Do you know how I know that? I distil them sometimes; I have a little distillation kit. And when you distil the pure spirit out of a plant, the oil, if you put that in a bottle and leave it there for five or six days, when you go back you don't see it you know, it disappear, so when you do that you have to capture it with a little sunflower oil or a little olive oil. So that's how I know that the plants have spirit and them have life, and they can talk to you, as you say. They can't talk to you word fi word, but they can communicate with you . . . The other

day, I never feel so good. I was really sick. So I'm there like
that . . .

A cricket screeching rises, becoming almost deafening.
I'm forced to lean in to hear this other tale . . .

And there are these herbs named piaba – man piaba and woman
piaba. The woman piaba call me . . . I was in Kingston, and it
called me and said to me, 'Why don't you drink me?' And I came
up and I start drinking the piaba and I feel much, much better. And
you know what that's about? Because I am seventy, my period stop
for years. But like my body lack oestrogen, and the piaba is a herb
that gives you oestrogen, so that is why it call me into it.

And do you talk to the plants them? Another thing I'm eager
to know.

Well, most time . . . Most time me a weed them, me talk to them.
Some of them, me say, 'Boy me nuh wa'an chop you down, you
know, but because you likkle bit unruly, me have to cut you back,'
and so on . . .

I find myself talking to the plants too, I offer . . .

And the thing about plants now, Miss Ivey proceeds to tell me,
if you picking plants, you don't pick it till the sun come up, and
you don't pick it after six o'clock, because they gone to sleep. Say for
example, somebody in your house get sick and you going to break
the plant after six, you have to talk to it, and tell the plant, 'Well,
this person is sick and I want you to help me, so I'm gonna break
you.' You can't just go bruk it after six, it's just sleeping . . . They
wake up at five o'clock in the morning and they go back to sleep by
six o'clock in the evening. It's a very unique world . . . Plants don't
like wicked people; plant nuh work with no evil spirit people. You
have plants what them use to work wid dem thing-de you know . . .

evil work . . . but them plant-de, me no really play with them.
Plants are very, very sensitive, simple as people see them.

After a while sitting on the veranda, Ivelyn invites me to
walk with her again through her garden, this time pointing
to the different plants, telling me the right angle from which
to photograph them.

This one is what we call the djonjo, good for people who suffer
from any form of haemorrhage . . .

   The piaba is a must-have for women going through
menopause; it's also great for calming nervous tension.

   This black Betty is one of the most powerful herbs inna the
herbal kingdom to make baths . . .

   The Mary Goules can pair with plantain . . . Many times, we
prepare herbs in odd numbers, but some plants can pair, like these
two . . . Her voice trails off . . .

   You know the thing that's going to kill out all the plants that
people need fi use to cure themselves? This Gramoxone . . . You
know the Gramoxone?

                                               Yeah, the pesticide.

The weed killer! A nuh pesticide you know, it's weed killer. When
they spray it and the other weed killer-dem, they kill everything,
and some bad bush come up, some different kind of bush come up
that you never see before. And them people-dem is so lazy that
they just love to spray . . . even if they planting a piece of
dasheen, they use the Gramoxone to weed it. What kind of
nonsense is that?! And it stay in the earth fi twenty-five years
after you use it 'e know . . .

                         And a it a give people cancer, nuh so?

Of course! You know how much people mi know dead from
using Gramoxone pan without anything over them nose? . . .
You see my yard: the leaves can stay there and the grass can
stay there till me ready to cut it and rake it, because a so the
earth supposed to stay. It's not supposed to stay the way you
think it fi stay.

In England, people would call someone like Miss Ivey a 'wild
gardener'.

Our conversation lasts just over an hour, after which I
back my vehicle out of Miss Ivey's narrow lane and head
down the hill. As I come out of the lane, I immediately
notice that to my right a river is running – flowing under
the road I'm now driving on. I'm caught between going
ahead and staring at the mood-elevating beauty of this
river rushing beneath me – how did I not notice it on my
way in? – but I shouldn't stare too much: I need to pay
attention to this narrow road. In places, it has holes that
are more like craters. Good thing I'm driving a 4 x 4 vehicle.
I can't imagine any car making it over these roads with its
front end intact. The roads are so rugged, I can't help but
think that they're not meant to be passable. They get
treacherous in places where you can look out from the car
and see the wide maw of a culvert, where the road's edge
has been eaten away by the rains. Better not drive here at
night, if you can avoid it.

The world here feels so unspoilt, a zone unto itself, and
I don't think I'm saying this because I already know the
history of the Maroons. This place is unexploited. You get
the distinct sense that it's meant to be. *Enclave* is the word
that comes to mind. The history of the Maroons is in the

air of the place, the physical lay of the land keeps an imprint of it – of those Africans who escaped surveillance, who formed kinship with the mountains and woodlands, living far away from the terrains exploited by the white European slave masters; who evaded recapture with such fierce, redoubtable resistance that they became feared; who preserved plant knowledge and healing. And the preservation of this history is integral to the Maroon identity today.

By the time I arrive in Port Antonio, I realise that it would be foolish to try to reach Coffee Grove this evening. It's almost 5 p.m. and the drive back is over four hours. I ring Hopeton, a friend who lives in nearby Three Hills, St Mary, to ask if I can spend the night at his place. He's happy to welcome a long-time friend tonight, to sip some rum with me while listening to reggae music, and I'm relieved to be able to break up the long journey. On the way to Hopeton, I stop on the roadside in Annotto Bay to buy jelly coconuts. I drink the water from the coconut cup, as we sometimes call the shell, then ask the vendor to *huks it up* for me so I can scoop up the soft jelly with the spoon that he'll have made by cutting off a strip of the husk with his sharp machete. I also buy jerk pork from a jerk shop along the roadside. Healthy food, but in England these types of vendors would not be operating, not even in summer; the *health and safety regulations* wouldn't allow it. I buy bottles of honey, pineapples, mangoes and other fruit, which I stash in the cardboard box at the back of my car; some of them are thank-you gifts for Hopeton.

On Hopeton's veranda in Three Hills, he and I have a good catch-up over some Guinness while looking out at the sun setting over his wild front yard. The food he's prepared for dinner – mackerel rundown accompanied by the tenderest boiled pumpkin I can ever remember eating – is heavenly, and after having another Guinness each, he takes me to a nearby bar where we hang around for a couple of hours, listening to the chunes from the sound system playing there. But I'm exhausted from the day's activities and soon I persuade him to return home so I can get some sleep.

I feel the breadth (and the breath) of the project I've taken on; the feeling emerges from the geographical distances I've just travelled. I'm thinking of all of Jamaica now in terms of its land and of how people live with it. I want to visit grungs all over the country, to know about how peasants use the land. For now, however, I'll settle for Coffee Grove, where I'll be returning in the morning.

It's well after noon when I leave Hopeton's the next day. I didn't fight the urge to have a lie-in or, later, to linger chatting with the good friend I hadn't seen in a few years. As a result, when I get back to Coffee Grove, it's already five o'clock. After unloading the car, I sit down to phone my wife and children back in Leeds. My little girls need reassurance that Daddy is all right. *When are you coming back, Daddy?* Leyla asks me. My two-year-old just says my name over and over again. *Yeah*, her only answer, is accompanied by a long, unending stare after I ask, *Are you all right?*, while Leyla, who's left the phone screen, is giggling and prancing around. I've been away from my family for nineteen days now and the pressure's getting too much to bear for my wife. I'm going to have to give a lot, do a lot, to make up for this when I get back. My wife has been very generous, accommodating my research in Coffee Grove, but she also runs a business.

Her parents sometimes help out with the children, but they live far away. It's a challenge. For the next half an hour after the phone call, I laze around the yard at Miss Rita's, thinking about all this and about what might have to give. I'm flying back to England in two days.

Wake up, leaves! So we can use you
as remedies taken under the orientation
of the doctor Òsanyìn, to whom
we shall pay the medical honorariums,
swearing never to deceive him.

—From the *sassanha*, Candomblé
ritual of 'waking' the plants

9.

Walking in England

That I have become 'middle class' is a fact I cannot deny. The very fact that I am experiencing 'leisure' for the first time underscores it. I have come into this moment, thinking these thoughts, because of where I came to live in Leeds, on the edge of a park and a small distance from the woods. For the first time in my life, I have enough money and material security to be able to *take my time*. To be able to take time off, to walk in the woods in the middle of a 'working day'. I want to take my time with the world, I simply want to be with things, I want to exit bourgeois ideology, exit the obsession with aspiring, accumulating possessions, gathering more and more things. But I realise that to do this – to give up the privilege of money and materials – is to be slammed by an inexorable system. There's no place – literally, no space – for someone who simply wants to be: without money, you must become a worker, and workers have no time.

I live in a new body, I have moved away from my childhood and the child I was. I have taken on a bourgeois body. *What is it to become the kind of body that one has hated?* I've adapted this question from a section of Édouard Louis' book *Combats et métamorphoses d'une femme* (*A Woman's Battles and Transformations*), in which the writer addresses his mother directly. He's just recounted an episode in which his impecunious mother, desperate to earn some cash and considering the increasingly comfortable financial situation of her son Édouard, the writer, offers to clean the latter's house in exchange for money. For Louis, this, unsurprisingly, is a source of shame. (So much of Louis' work hovers around the shame and violence of class, around what Bourdieu calls 'class habitus'.) He tries to penetrate the dynamic at work in this interaction with his mother:

> *When I was a child with you, in the village, and I saw well-to-do people, the mayor, the little castellans, the owners of the pharmacy, of the grocery store, most of the time I hated them, because I saw in them all the privileges that I didn't have access to.*
>
> *I hated their bodies, their freedom, their money, the ease of their movements.*
>
> *If you asked me to become my housekeeper that day, does that mean that I became this body?*

The shock and the shame of this moment awaken him to the cost of changing class.

The novelty of living on the edge of a park with all its woodlands has prompted these thoughts. Suddenly I'm realising how much 'leisure' is political. On the one hand, the possibility of tenderness in the current world – where existing while Black entails so much violence – means defending my right to slowness, to unobligated time, to quiet, to what some people will describe as 'leisure'. It's the kind of lifestyle that's only recently been made possible for me. The possibility of tenderness is also a form of refusal. The refusal to accept that the 'nature' allotted to me must always be something brutal. Or angry. A refusal of the need to be righteous. By 'righteous', I mean the perpetual need to prove my worthiness to thrive, to deserve the access to space that whiteness grants its carriers. Overcoming the internalised sensations of erasure developed over decades, I'm now intentionally allowing myself time, space and moments of 'leisure', and it's my response to a culture which has always denied that to bodies like mine. I insist on viewing my body as the right one in the right place.

These are my thoughts as I prepare to meet up with a Black walking group in Huddersfield. On this last Thursday of June, I'm meeting them for the first time. It's also my first time 'walking' since my return from Jamaica.

We meet at a parking lot in the centre of Huddersfield. A crowd of retired West Indian migrants, or their descendants, some of them elderly, most of them men. Andrea, who invited me along, is one of only two women, the other being Cynthia. They are both from Carriacou, a tiny island in the eastern Caribbean, linked to Grenada. In fact, the entire group hails from Carriacou. I say 'hails from Carriacou', knowing full well that a number of them were born in England of immigrant Carriacou parents. Some, like McDonald and Rocky, who must be in their early seventies, came to England in the 1960s when they were children, part of the Windrush Generation.

They offer me a warm welcome, each one telling me her or his name; I won't remember all of them, of course, but I get to hear their accents, whose lilts and vibrancy put me in the memory of home. Some of them have poles, which to me says 'old age', limbs no longer very nimble, joints no longer very supple.

I am here to learn from these West Indian elders, to gain drops of wisdom, but also simply for the pleasure of sharing the experience of walking with them. They're all drawn here, like me, by the need to go out into the countryside and claim the space as their own.

From the car park, we take a steep downward path among bushes and the dark, cavernous spaces of an English wood in late June. Its felted silence, an effect of the thickness of the foliage, feels protective, evoking to me, as always, the feeling of a womb, or what I think a womb might feel like. I take joy in being with my fellow walkers – newly found companions who resemble me – in the wood's submarine greenness: a group of Black people going for a long walk in the English countryside, something I have never before seen with my own eyes.

I begin trying to identify plants, to look, at least, to my left and right at what lies on the ground. I want to actively pay attention to English plants, to their names and qualities. I think that plants must, like us, have an 'identity'. I'd never been very curious, up to now, about the 'identities' of English plants, which had always seemed impenetrable to me. The sense that I would ultimately fail to connect with them has always prevailed; it's a feeling of foreignness, of having landed in a different landscape. I feel, always, that the land in which we live knows our bodies, that we are also known by it. Regardless of whether that's true, I've sometimes thought it might be impossible to truly know a landscape that's not the one in which you've grown up, the one in which you've moved, lived, spent your time. There's something deeply sensual, almost sacrificial, in this idea – that you give something, leave something in the soil, even as the soil penetrates you and changes your being. In an actual sense, this *does* happen: we are made of our environments. They enter us, shape us and change us, in the most physical ways.

Which is why I'm terrified of the idea of staying indoors; the idea of being anxious about going outdoors, about walking the land where one lives, as an immigrant, a foreigner, a 'guest'. What happens when we do not allow the earth to get into us, to penetrate us?

I walk behind limping Raymond with his walking pole and listen to the conversations taking place. The theme is, unsurprisingly, home – news about the children living in England, news of the elders and siblings in Carriacou, updates on building projects and extensions happening back in the West Indies, where many of them dream of returning. I keep my eye on the bush for anything that might surge out of the monotonous green of bilberry shrubs, nettles and young oaks. The flora on these walking trails may be impoverished by the footfall of urban rambling, by centuries of forest management. When I draw level with Andrea – deliberately, I've mostly been bringing up the rear – I ask her whether she has any knowledge of the herbs found in these woods, whether there are any she knows about or has made use of for medicinal purposes. Andrea seems surprised by my question. At first, her answer seems categorical: she doesn't know of any. Disappointed, I continue to hope that something will surface from her memory. Perhaps she does have some knowledge of these herbs, something lying beneath the surface, that will be sparked by our conversations.

After the initial stretch of forest, we re-emerge into the urban space. There's nothing that reawakens you to urban everyday reality as much as the sight of a McDonald's, the neon yellow of its big 'M' hardly separable from the chain of large, imposing signs on the façades of the stores that form a giant shopping complex – Bensons for Beds, Dunelm furniture store, Argos . . . From the car park, we've walked through the sloping wood for about twenty minutes, before emerging here on Beck Road, beside Huddersfield's Ringway industrial estate. But after just twenty minutes spent in the silence of the wood, even this sight – the expanse of land on which shopping offers the promise of an almost erotic gratification – has become strange again. It's as if you've gained new eyes, the re-encounter with the urban space, the massive concourses of shops and their enormous signs, becoming a shock, defamiliarising – in the same way, probably, as the scene of us along this stretch of road, walking together, equipped with hiking paraphernalia, is abnormal to the people looking on from the queue of cars waiting at a traffic light. Through this queue, we cross over to the other side of the street before making our way back into the green – another patch of woodland within the city that Andrea and the other walkers refer to simply as 'the steps'.

Up the many steps we go, Rocky asking me how it's going. I tell him that I'm looking – I've been looking all along. I can only identify spikenard and bilberry (my four-year-old daughter is an expert at foraging for these, identifying the shrubs from far away), nettles, many oaks. *That's already good*, I reassure myself. Yet I can't help but wonder: What if Mama were here? How would this walk unfold with her by my side? What if she had lived in England? Would her curiosity for the plants have been subdued, like mine? It's difficult to imagine, but would she have stifled it? Could migration have had that effect on her? Or would she be eagerly scanning the bush, as she did in Coffee Grove?

And my mother. She's the same age as some of these Carriacouans. All of a sudden, I'm imagining going for walks with her, like this, in Yorkshire. Surely she'd also be going on her own, or with people who look like her. Wouldn't she be scouring the landscape for wildflowers, foraging, snapping pictures?

I shuffle along to get beside McDonald. As he mounts the stairs, we talk about plants. He speaks about the intimate folk knowledge that his Carriacouan people have of their plants, which seems quite similar to what I've found in Jamaica. And what does it mean for us that we haven't got access to this knowledge of the plants here, I ask, a question as much for myself as for him.

It have stuff that's good for things, but we don't know them, he says, resignedly.

Perhaps it hasn't been easy to know those things till now, I reply. *Perhaps it's easier for your grandkids to know that sort of stuff.*

Then Phil comes along beside us, a white man hailing from Huddersfield, the only white person present in this group. He's retired from a career consulting in the creative industries. Phil's curious about what I do. I explain that I'm writing a book that narrates my childhood in rural Jamaica and my experience of walking with my grandmother. *I talk about her way of walking*, I say to him, *about her relationship to plants, trees and the woodlands*, as a stepping-off point for a journey of recollection and discovery.

And what is this way of walking? he asks.

It involves stopping, looking and listening, an interactive process, I reply. This way of walking helps me to detangle the word *nature*, and to unpack the strange intersections of race, class and time that are contained in it, even as I embark on a journey of reconnecting with key plants from those childhood walks. This is how I describe my book to Phil, who's an expert on English plants. The book, I tell him, is about plants, but beyond that, it's about asserting the right to know this land, to take my time in a land that's not originally mine, but which, I have to admit, is now 'home'.

Well, it's a two-way street, isn't it, he says, after digesting the thought for a few seconds. *It's about Black people going into the countryside, but it's also about the countryside seeing Black people . . . Everybody deserves to be seen.*

We converse about the knowledge and passions inherited from our respective herbalist grandmothers, and I share with him a list of some of the plants I've encountered or rediscovered in Jamaica. We compare notes, Phil asking questions about Jamaica, me silently realising that a whole world of possibilities has been opened up to me through the meeting of this man via the Black walking group. There are two kinds of riches here: the joy of walking with fellow Black people; and the wonder and gift, the undreamed-of gift, of forming kinship with the land in Yorkshire.

Phil recommends that I read the *Complete Herbal* by Nicholas Culpeper. *Proper folk knowledge of herbs*, he says, *beyond a mere scientific perspective.* We speak about the decline of herbalist knowledge in English culture; about how rare it is to meet someone like him today, someone who has such intimate knowledge of the plants. When I read *Culpeper's Complete Herbal*, I am indeed fascinated by the language used to describe plants and their virtues. For example, speaking about sweet sedge, the author writes: 'The spicy bitterness of the root of this plant bespeaks it as a strengthener of the stomach and head and therefore may fitly be put into any composition of that intention.' *Strengthener* – this is the type of word that my Jamaican people use to talk about herbs. It's evident that this description, suggesting intimate acquaintance, comes from a familiarity with what different plants do and how they function, from an inherited knowledge.

After two hours of walking, we're in Marsden, a village lying on the eastern flank of the Pennines. It's an area filled with sandstone walkways, 'millstone grit', as they call it here, and where you'll often see houses with roofs made of sandstone slates. This type of rock is obviously abundant in the area. You only need to look at the landscape: the stone steps and pathways that likely played a crucial role in transporting goods and accessing pastures for livestock; the stone walls that form boundaries and enclosures; the houses made of sandstone; the mills whose chimneys still rise impressively from this section of the Colne Valley. From where we stand on the hillcrest, we can see two textile mills, imposing sandstone edifices. Disused now, they were once significant to this region in the era of flax spinning and textile manufacturing.

The northern region of England, particularly Lancashire and Yorkshire, played a pivotal role in Britain's Industrial Revolution, with the textile industry serving as its cornerstone. While wool production had deep roots in the area, the arrival of cotton in the eighteenth century heralded an epochal shift. The cotton woven in this region between the eighteenth and mid-nineteenth centuries arrived as a direct result of colonialism: none of it was grown here, yet by the mid-nineteenth century, Britain was supplying half the world's cotton cloth, using cotton produced in the warm climates of India and Egypt, and in the Southern United States, where it was produced using slave labour. Before that, cotton had also come from the West Indies, but by the late eighteenth century the slave plantations there had almost completely divested themselves of it to focus instead on sugar.

Cotton weaving, centred in Manchester and surrounding towns like Rochdale, Oldham and Stockport, thrived due to the region's damp climate, which facilitated cotton processing. Conversely, the Calder Valley, where we currently are, primarily focused on wool production, with limited cotton-textile manufacturing. While some cotton weaving existed in places like Hebden Bridge, wool remained the dominant textile in the area.

Standing here, you really get the sense of Marsden as a mill village, and now Phil begins to speak about this very thing:

These enormous mills, he says, *are still owned by the family that built them, the Crowther family. They ran the whole village. They've just had some money from the Levelling Up Fund to actually do up that whole mill . . .*

What will 'doing up' this mill involve, I wonder, but I don't ask this out loud. *All that tile work is impressive,* I say instead. *I'm always admiring of that skill and artistry.*

Soon we're walking across Marsden Moor, opening and closing lambing hurdles and sheep-handling gates; reading the signs to dog owners about keeping their animals on leads; crossing bridges. And, as always, the stone walls stand out. The simple deftness of their construction is the element of the landscape here that evokes memories of the Jamaican countryside for me.

Walking at a variable pace, I get to talk to different people at different times.

There's lots of nettle here . . . I remark out loud. *Anybody know what, if anything, it's good for?*

Well, yes, I tell people how good the nettle is, one of the Carriacouan men lets out. *Good for hay fever, except when it's flowering.* Knowledge of the plants, after all, despite what they say.

Phil chimes in with his lore: a dock leaf rubbed on a nettle sting can alleviate it; then something about nigella . . . I resolve to visit him at his home at some point, sit in his garden and listen to him pour forth his knowledge of local plants.

Suddenly the rain starts coming down. The weather had already turned grey the moment we entered Marsden Moor. Slanted needles of rain hit me from left and right. All at once, I'm cold. It's wet. How could this sunny June weather have turned miserable so quickly? I look down at my shoes: bright yellow Adidas Gazelles. My flat soles become threateningly slippery now that the rain is falling. *Them there's fashion shoes,* says Andrea, poking fun.

Always carry a little covering in your bag, adds Rocky.

Well, that was this, I say, pointing to my long-sleeve military overshirt. I have only that over my T-shirt, whereas all the others are wearing raincoats. These people are prepared! I put today's attire down to inexperience.

You've gotta be prepared on the moors, Cynthia says. *The weather changes so fast: sunny in the morning and by the time you get on the moors . . . oh my Gawd* – at this point her accent comes out strong – *big snow!* With this, Rocky, Errol and the crew start to laugh, looking at me. Not even a head covering or an umbrella here. I own walking boots, but I didn't even think of wearing them.

Not even a hat, Jason! Errol joins in; it's fair-enough banter.

I hope one o' you have some rum in you bag for me to rub up myself. I keep it rolling: *Poor planning, I do everything too last-minute.*

Coming off the moor, we find ourselves descending a steep road. Waters Road, a sign shows. Another one indicates a place named Hey Green House. Funny-sounding name, I think to myself, supposing it to be some amusement place for kids. But then a blue plaque on the stone wall bounding the property informs me that here, around 1890, a water-powered generator was installed to provide the first electricity to light a house in the Colne Valley: *Hey Green House and the generator were owned by Joseph Crowther, a prominent mill-owner.*

This is obviously relatively interesting, declares Andrea, with a suddenly posh inflection, and we both laugh out loud at the performative Englishness of her statement. I observe that it's the same mill-owning family that Phil mentioned earlier as we looked down into the valley.

At around the two-and-a-half-hour mark, there's a break for group stretching and breathing exercises along the trail. The exercises loosen up my body and I instantly begin to feel my blood flowing more energetically; it's exhilarating.

There is no further discussion of plants with the Carriacouans. I can't say I observe much in the way of plants along our walk. I find the cattle farms more noticeable, and the paddocks for horses, with their varicoloured cloths over their bodies. The horses have such care meted out to them; they look luxurious, meticulously groomed. I can't help but notice the times when our path leads us out of wooded spaces back onto the main roads. It drives home the reality that there is not enough public land to walk on for three hours, the walkable spaces are limited; at the same time, it says something about the determination of this group to walk and to keep on walking. Errol tells me that he walks four times a week. He's convinced that if he didn't do

this – *if I did sit down on the couch at home not doing anything,*
he says – he would be in bad health.

I accept now that there probably won't be a lot of discussion about plants here; I might not get from them the big revelations or insights I'd hoped for – West Indians living with plants in Britain, and whatnot. But it doesn't matter, because I'm getting something really valuable from this group. What it gives me is the gift of seeing Black people walking through the woods, through the green spaces where our feet seldom tread in this country. Every now and again, I turn around to look at the line of people, and just the visual does wonders for my mind.

But it's not just the chance to see these Black folks walking, though that's amazing; it's also the fact of being a part of it. Being in these spaces with people from the Caribbean awakens all sorts of feelings in my body. Being able to walk with people who look like you, and with whom you share a historical experience, means there are so many things you're aware of that you don't need to explain. There's a sense of recognition that shields you, fortifies you – the result is that when you encounter white British people in the forest, you perceive in a whole different way the gaze coming at you: I've never had the experience before of so many white people – almost everybody – smiling, exchanging a laugh, cracking some joke, saying some kind word. They're meeting a group of people, rather than an isolated Black man. And their bodies, oh their bodies, how open they are! How devoid of hostility. How open and engaged, welcoming of conversation, of us. I have not seen any hostility or fear today. Maybe it's also the in-group markers of hiking poles, walking shoes and trekking paraphernalia that say 'British', enough to trump colour in this particular context. Then there's the average age of the group – pretty high – which makes us less threatening. Regardless, walking within the group redefines who I am on a walk through the green spaces. If only I could have that feeling all the time.

Two weeks later, I drop by Phil's place for a visit. He and his wife, Deryn, warmly welcome Leyla and me into their home. Over lunch, our conversation meanders until Phil, clearing the table, announces, *Now, let's move on to more serious matters.* With his granddaughter and Leyla happily occupied inside, the three of us venture into his sun-drenched garden.

It's the second week of July, a warm summer's day casting a gentle glow over the lush greenery. Phil's garden, though not expansive, is meticulously organised, reminding me of Congolin's farm. From rows of vibrant vegetables to a green-house filled with exotic treasures like bananas and grapes, every corner tells a story.

Phil points proudly to his rosemary plant, at which point I share its Jamaican moniker. *Memory weed*, I say.

His eyes light up with curiosity. *Did you ever hear an explanation for that?* he asks. Explaining its significance, we share a moment of realisation – across both our cultures, rosemary symbolises memory and remembrance.

English folklore, Deryn says, *advises that you slip it into the pocket of an unfaithful lover to help them remember their vow.*

As we stroll, Phil imparts his gardening wisdom, from brewing comfrey tea to the historical origins of lungwort and mugwort. Each plant holds a tale, connecting us to the tapestry of English folk medicine, one whose richness I'm discovering more and more, thanks in no small part to my association with Phil.

Approaching a low-growing plant with silver-speckled

leaves, Phil identifies it as pulmonaria. *Well, pulmonaria just sounds like pulmonary, I remark.*

His grin widens. *Exactly!* he agrees, recounting its use in English folk medicine. *Traditionally, people used to use that for a lung treatment because they thought that the leaves looked like lungs . . . In England, it was called lungwort. And it was used for lungs, but only because it looked like a lung.*

English folk medicine, I think to myself, pretty much resembles Jamaican traditional plant lore when it comes to the naming of herbs according to their medicinal usage. It's like search mi heart, fever grass, memory weed . . . Lungwort is literally *the lung plant.* Wort is simply the Anglo-Saxon word for 'plant'. Now, thanks to my walks in the Yorkshire countryside, conversations with Phil and my reading of English herbal books, I've started to enjoy English plant names and delving into English plant lore. As a sound, *mugwort* is harsh and fascinating in equal measure. Definitely not suavely English. I find fascinating the simplicity of the name: mugwort is literally *the plant that you put in the mug.*

As we amble through the garden, Phil's voice takes on a storyteller's cadence, drawing me into a fascinating tale of beer-making lore.

Traditionally, he begins, *the wort was the key ingredient in beer-making, responsible for giving flavour. Back then, before the arrival of hops, brewers relied on a blend of herbs, which was also known as the wort.*

He pauses, his eyes gleaming with intrigue. *And that's where it gets interesting,* he continues. *You see, this practice of brewing beer was steeped in mystique. Also, it was women who did it. This was a domain that they had control over. So you can understand how the figure of the brewster eventually became associated with witchcraft.* According to Phil, the brewster's mysterious power over the brew was perceived as a threat.

I lean in as he shares this tale about the brewsters – powerful women who in medieval times wielded secret recipes and commanded respect. *Beer-making was their domain,* he explains. *And beer was more than just a beverage – it was essential, healthier than water in those days.*

As he speaks, vivid images of brewsters stirring their cauldrons dance in my mind. If Phil's tale is true, this would be another case of male anxiety fuelling the patriarchal policing of women. Was the medieval brewster indeed the origin of the image of the witch at her cauldron, as he was suggesting?

I envision the scene – broomsticks protruding from doorways, signalling that the beer was ready. It's a tale that resonates with history and magic. I'm drawn in by its intrigue.

As we amble through Phil's domain, I find myself captivated by his knowledge of the plants and the profound satisfaction he derives from nurturing the earth. Each stroke of his hand, each tender moment with the soil, is a testament to his intimate bond with the land.

I begin to envision myself embarking on a similar journey – a journey of cultivation and connection. The mere thought ignites a spark of possibility, kindling questions of a life intertwined with the soil of England. Lucile and I often muse about finding a home with ample gardening space, a sanctuary where we can cultivate our own patch of earth. For in soil, we find a common thread that unites us all – a universal canvas upon which all of life is painted.

As Phil shares his insights, I am struck by the universality of our relationship with earth. Though its nature may vary, its essence remains unchanged – a source of nourishment, both physical and spiritual, capable of sustaining life wherever it may take root.

In a quiet moment alone with Phil, I broach the question that has long lingered in my mind – a question of belonging, of connection. Can I, as a foreigner, forge a bond with the soil of England? It's a daunting prospect, one that has eluded me for too long. But as I voice my doubts, I am met with Phil's unwavering optimism, his belief in the transformative power of curiosity and determination. Perhaps, he suggests, the key lies not in replicating his methods, but in embracing the journey with an open mind and a willing heart.

Prowling . . .

local existence

local seeds

Prowling

the possibility of tenderness

within the soil

of transplantation

10.

Mama's Salindine

It's a while before I actually find the grave. A number of tombs have been added to the churchyard cemetery since October 2012, when Mama was buried. In the past, I could easily identify so many: Pastor Barrett, Mother Scille, Sister Caro . . . those elders who were already old when I was a child. But now there are names I don't even recognise or remember. By searching hard and calling on spatial memory, I eventually spot Mama's tomb. The inscription on the marble headstone has been almost completely erased; the lilac paint from the sides is gone as well. No wonder it was hard to find. Does Mommy know the state the grave is in? In the early-afternoon sun, I'm forced to squint to look out over the fields bounding the church, but the church wall casts its shade over the tombs. I stand in that shade and observe the butterflies twirling in the large castor bean tree hanging over a set of tombs that includes Mama's. Although I'm frustrated by the grave's neglect, the sight of the swirling butterflies brings a sense of calm. Gradually, the initial frustration wanes in the midst of their graceful dance.

Hello, Mama, I'm here, I'm back with you after many long journeyings. Are you satisfied with what I've become? I ask into the air. Saying this, I begin to consider the journeys: the Bahamas, Montreal, Oxford, Paris, Leeds . . . I've seldom come to see this grave since the burial a decade ago; I reckon this is only my second time. *Reckon*: early senses of this word, the dictionary tells me, 'included "give an account of items received" . . . which gave rise to the notion of "calculation" '. Perhaps I haven't come more often because I wasn't ready; maybe I thought I needed to have something to show for myself, something to count up, to present to Mama.

Whether I realised it or not, coming to stand at Mama's grave is a way of measuring time. And what have I done with my time? Have all my trips been worth it? Was leaving Mama behind, going far away from her in those years before she died, worth it? As she lay six weeks on a hospital bed getting ready to die – 'travelling', as we say here – I was in Paris, partying, living it up with my Erasmus friends, on my student exchange from Oxford. Returning now, I say, simply, *sorry* – for failing to grasp the extent of your efforts in safeguarding my happiness, shielding me from the world's harshness. Yet, I also return to pose a question: *Are you proud of me, Mama?* Because, despite it all, you gave me the space to dream. A *reckoning*, then, of the journey taken: for so long, all I could see this place as was somewhere to run from. Progress was outside, over the oceans, in Europe's marbled cities. While I did love you, I was running from you, trying to hide you from the world.

It's February 2023 and I find myself back in Coffee Grove. The days of the pandemic, which was still raging during my last visit, now feel so far away. Back then, my grandmother's house was rotting. It felt like a second death. There are things that are meant to keep you alive even after you're dead. A house with its contents is one of them. The sanctuary of the home is where the departed one touches us

through the senses – they make themselves felt as a presence. How do we preserve our dead without the heirlooms,
without the material, without the mass? What are we
allowed or able to keep as we form new generations? Are
our belongings mainly immaterial things, the ghosts we live
amongst, who share their lives with us? This question haunts
me as I think about decline and degeneration, about rot;
about the wasp nests that have infested the cornices of this
house, about the duck ants eating away at the roof. As I
think, too, about my mother, who is now fixing the roof of
the little old house in preparation for living in it; the moment
will be one in which she will, for the first time in her life, live
in a house that belongs to her.

Corpus. The body is both a presence and an absence. My
grandmother's handbag, her clothing, her brush, her brooch,
her handwritten letter, all carry the presence of her body.
Objects become stand-ins for the body. What happens to
memory when there is no *corpus* to 'support' it? When the
bodies of things cannot be preserved? This is the fate of the
'poor'. We keep on losing stuff. We are unable to preserve
and accumulate. Our cycles of ownership are short. Often
we cannot hold on to land because we have never 'owned' it.
The poor lack the money to preserve stuff.

I've stepped inside the house now. My feet seem so big, my
footsteps so heavy, like a giant's within this small house,
whose ceilings seem to have come down to meet my head.
My shoulders feel broad, and the place that's everything to
me, from which I spring, now feels distant, almost beyond
reach, though I'm standing in it; I know that this is my place,
yet I struggle to feel at home in it the way my younger self
did. What name do we have for that feeling you get when a

place feels foreign while also being deeply familiar? There's distance between my body and this dwelling, yet it remains the genesis of my journey. And my eye has that bed fixed in it. I know the story it represents: *When I bought it, from the year of when, the big money I saved when I got my first work, when I came from Vere to here, that was when me and Joe Morgan married, and I buy this bed, and it older than you mother.* I scan the room and see that barrel with all the crockery in it, the crockery that must not be touched, so precious. *Who sent this barrel?*

One time, many years ago, before I was born, or perhaps in the days just after I was born, a barrel was sent from some Sister This or That whom Mama had helped to go to 'Merica. She helped her, did everything, for the woman could not read, even got her papers for her, and in a gesture of acknowledgement, this Sister This or That sent her a barrel. The details have long slipped out of memory, but somebody sent a barrel. Barrels have a particular importance in our history since the era of the mass migration of Jamaicans to 'the Mother Country', and to the United States and Canada, in the second half of the twentieth century. For a long time, they've been how migrant parents and loved ones care for their family back home, sending provisions, including food, clothing, school supplies, household goods and treats (sweets, exotic canned fruits and food), that are not available there. For this reason, barrels can become hugely symbolic of a family's status in peasant districts like Coffee Grove: they're a sign you have relatives 'in foreign' – that alone is a huge deal – who remember you and are doing well enough to be able to lavish you with the wondrous foreign wares, clothes and delicacies of a barrel.

Again, I do not know where this barrel came from. To be

honest, now that I think about it, perhaps this barrel was not even addressed to us. Perhaps, for the practical reason of storing some of her things, Mama had merely acquired it from the people who did receive it from abroad. I also remember dreaming up a fictional tale of well-off cousins in foreign who were close to Mama and who showed their love by packing and shipping a barrel of fancy foreign things; it was a fantasy story of privilege I made up as a kid. In reality, we had no such person overseas; the things that Sister Vads sent me, such as the toy helicopter and a few ganzies (our word for T-shirt), arrived in parcels that Mama would receive at the postal agency. Yet this barrel has all the things in it that you must do this or that with *when I dead*. It was my privilege to hear: *This is for you and this is for your mother when I dead. I want you to know 'bout it, is only you I want to get it, nobody else, when I dead.*

All the untouchables – the pressure cooker, the chinaware, the tea set that's even better than the one in the cabinet, the things you only need to *know* you have. So much is for the display, the embrace, so much is a series of monuments to our right to own things, to our claim on wealth and leisure. So much is a curation, as Alice Walker might remind us – in the ordering, in the tending, in the order and the care – an expression of the suppressed creative pursuit. But there's also a tenderness, a marking of the moment, some kind of deep gratitude, if not to the *wutliss*, ungrateful people that you helped up out of the dirt to reach a foreign, then at least to God that you've acquired something in this life, something you can pass on to your child and grandchild.

Yet, in this house, things that should be heirlooms are disintegrating, are becoming dispersed, discarded. Currently, the new roof is being constructed. New windows and doors will be fitted. But the house has been left exposed during the replacement of the roof. The rain has come in, causing the barrel cover to rust; inside, the books and pieces of cloth that are left are damp and musty. The beautiful Formica dresser is collapsing, soggy with rainwater. There are pools of water on the ground. The builder has taken no care to protect the house's contents. Perhaps Mommy did not have the means to organise having Mama's old things protected, and so resigned herself to fate. So often she has resigned herself. Over the years, poverty has created in her a mindset of resignation. When you become resigned to fate, you prefer not to see the rot, the disintegration. It's easier not to see it, easier to go on, move ahead, to carry out the actions considered vital. Preserving heirlooms and the belongings of the dead, thinking about accumulation, about 'patrimony', these become far less important, if not impossible. The poor have no patrimony. Not here. Not if by 'patrimony' we mean objects passed down, stored. As I watched my grandmother's things rot and slowly disappear, I understood that our heritage exists in traces, if not in immaterial ways, in feelings carried deeply in the body.

It is true that Mommy has saved a few things by taking them away from the duck-ant-infested house and carrying them to her own rented home in Mandeville. In Mommy's home, I've seen Mama's mahogany cabinet, one of the most precious things of all; her tea set in bone china; her enamel pail and chimmy; her enamel kitchenware; the sole photo I ever saw in Mama's house, one of her favourite brother, Ronald, with Bertha, his wife; a handwritten letter from this brother residing in England – he arrived there in 1952. I'm comforted by this. It is not what the French call *patrimoine* and which the English translate as 'heritage', since the dispersal works against this very notion; the objects are scattered away from the location to which they belong, and gone also is the feeling of legacy, of accumulation, that one associates with the upper classes. But somehow, this feeling of dispersal feels emblematic of our lives – of mine and of Mama's. And this is what I'm observing in this museum called 'Mama's house'. The symbols of myself, my life and my travelling, the distances I've travelled and all the roads and improvised paths I've come through, this is *it*, here, looking back at me.

I can't get over the bed, the bed older than my mother. There's a smaller one on the other side of the partition, the cloth-covered wooden frame that seemed so solid in my childhood but which looks flimsy now; that single bed was mine, and no doubt it had been my mother's as well.

An old grip lies wistfully on this
more than fifty-year-old bed,
this bed that has always been,
and from which I spring.

It lies faithfully packed
with the garments of one who's to depart.

There have been a million partings.

The old grip inherited
from some old Sister This or That
lies filled with the garments of a sumptuous
journey. See the carefully,

lovingly folded fabric
of the cardigan that has no age,
the pale wonder of the timeless sweater.

You've got to understand how to read certain gestures. A fold, for instance. My grandmother attached so much meaning to the act of folding a piece of clothing. Folding shows the care that one takes, the thankfulness; it's a way of cultivating the feeling of luxury, of dwelling on it. Folding is an act of love, a ritual, an affirmation of dignity and pride. This care is what Alice Walker calls 'respect for the possibilities'. This care is a manifestation of our grandmothers' suppressed creative spark, of their desire to dream. The fold strikes me now, as it lies wistfully on this bed, as an emblem, a physical extension of Mama, a touchstone of memory. A fold made by her lives on in this moment; she clings to it. It becomes a vestige of her body, the *corpus* that remains present in myriad ways, even in my mother making her own folds, as she will, reminding me of *this one* lying before me; it is still Mama's fold.

The dresser was the control centre of Mama's bedroom. It was important to smell good and the dresser enabled this. Smelling good was a source of pride. A dab behind the ear with Mama's perfume, by her hand. It was priceless. Didn't matter that we were poor. But actually, 'poor' is an affect – an affect that the grown folks in Coffee Grove didn't have. That word was never mentioned.

Then there was the Vaseline in the hair . . .
the Purelene cocoa butter lotion
Pond's face cream

olive oil
talcum powder
the ceramic figurines
the radio
the crochet doilies
the hairpins
the perfume again
the mirror
the design of the dresser . . . white lacquered chipboard. Its
  curvaceous shape.

How Mama would oil me down at that dresser before we
went to church! This need to smell good was akin to the
pride she vested in her appearance, in how she presented
herself to the world. The sentiment mirrored the impera-
tive of keeping a clean yard, which Mama would sweep with
bur bush or coconut boughs. *Cleanliness is next to godliness*,
she would often say. Sweeping our yards with bur bush and
coconut boughs is also bush technology; it's something we
internalise from the moment of our childhood. For country
folk like Mama, cleanliness of body and surroundings is
often an obsession, and the first generations who travelled
to England in the forties, fifties and sixties were often
shocked by the relative disregard the English had for this
degree of tidiness. The English could never understand the
meaning of this kind of care – the rigidities and pieties of
which can be stifling – for what lay behind it was a preservation of humanness. They had never had to contend for this
and so could not understand it.

When Mama's flower garden produced plants that she
could cut, she'd gather some, put them in a vase and place
them on the dresser. They complemented the Christmas

cards also put to stand on the dresser, which remained there for the whole year, or beyond. Mama often mentioned her determination to have some place of her own, where she could go and come, a place not owned by the bank. When she separated from my grandfather, she had nothing, and she built this one-room house, *my little one-room*, she said. There was pride in that. I saw it expand to take on a dining room, then, later, it grew another room as a kitchen, and yet another room as a bathroom. Until then, Mama had had her bath outside, in a zinc cupboard behind the one-room house, in the cock-crowing, lamp-lit air of dusk in Coffee Grove. While she performed this routine, after my bath on the back steps, as the sun poured out its final gold dust, I would get dressed and get ready for bed. Perhaps there'd be time for a walk over to the barbecue, where Brother B sat looking out into the blinding juice of the sun, chewing a grass straw.

A piece from Jacqueline Bishop's History at the Dinner Table, *a series of twelve printed plates exhibited at the British Ceramics Biennial in Stoke-on-Trent, September–October 2021.*

I'm looking at photos of Jacqueline Bishop's 'alternative' dinner service, a series of painted china she designed for the British Ceramics Biennial in Stoke-on-Trent in the autumn of 2021. I first saw the china in a *Financial Times* article. The pieces are striking, and like the best artwork, they mess with our sense of the familiar, alter our viewing reality. And yet there's something about them that is disturbing. It's the way they seem to re-enact trauma. The scenes are violent, and it's not a violence that you can turn away from. The object is intimate, near; these are tea sets – what could be nearer and more intimate than the things you eat and drink from? One plate shows an unclothed enslaved woman, tied to something that's outside the viewing frame; her body seems almost suspended, her toes barely touching the ground. I imagine that the cord around her bound hands is tied to a tree. This is a dish. Something to eat from, and Bishop has brought this image of terror so near. There is no doubt that this is what she wants to do, to render violence intimate, but she's also disrupting the image of the china as something genteel, smooth, fine. She's disrupting the image of propriety, gentility and manners, an image so distant from the reality of the trade in and ownership of African flesh on the plantations of the Americas, so distant from the systemic poverty, social abjection and neglect of the Black majority that is its lasting legacy.

Bishop's china makes me think of Mama's. That tea set in the barrel and the one in the cabinet. I learned the word *chinaware* at the same time as learning that it was not a thing of the everyday. It was for the special occasion. I subsequently learned just how elusive the 'special occasion' was. So elusive that it never came round. Mama and I would never have an occasion to drink together from that tea set, or, say, drink together with guests or friends stopping by, or with distant family who were visiting. Our occasions for drinking never corresponded to the level that would warrant the use of her china. I understood that having the chinaware was about simply *having* it, about it being there. Its value was also the spectacle of its ownership. I observed this over and over, in the houses I frequented as a child on that dirt road in Coffee Grove, and later in the backstreets of Porus. The tea sets and the bone china, even the china that was not real china, were for special occasions only, forever locked inside the cabinet that no child could touch or go near. They were about the dignity of having something and the pride in being able to display it. This proper drinking of tea conveyed the entitlement our parents and grandparents felt to what was called 'leisure' in the chilly hat-and-coat-wearing, umbrella-carrying clime of England, but also in the households of backra, the local light-skinned elite, right here in Jamaica.

Bishop's images place horror against the backdrop of flora, flipping familiar narratives of gentility, landscape and leisure in her gold-rimmed porcelain collection. What more potent symbol exists of the enigmatic allure of the Caribbean islands than their lush landscapes – their soil, their flora? These breathtaking vistas have borne witness to terror, yet they remain a canvas upon which our ancestors have painted their creativity, defiantly nurturing their artistic spirit despite the shackles of generations past, which sought to extinguish their creative spark.

As an illustration, I need look no further than my mother and her plants, or Mama and her flowers placed in the vase. It is the extravagant cultivation, the fierce, purposeful defence of her body's right to beauty. I think, now, that Mama's beautification of her surroundings with plants, her love of plant cultivation, may evoke, too, some idea of what people call 'leisure' – some insistence on dreaming, on the right to feed the creative spirit. The kind of care that she practised with her hands feeds freedom dreams – hers, mine, my mother's.

Recently, while rereading Toni Morrison's *The Bluest Eye*, I found myself captivated by the following excerpt, as it evoked so well, for me, what I've just described as my peasant people's *insistence on dreaming*. Linking this African American reality, which Morrison conveys so masterfully, to my Jamaican one, I am able to appreciate this impulse as one common to our African diaspora:

> Knowing that there was such a thing as the outdoors bred in us a hunger for property, for ownership. The firm possession of a yard, a porch, a grape arbour. Propertied black people spent all their energies, all their love, on their nests. Like frenzied, desperate birds, they overdecorated everything; fussed and fidgeted over their hard-won homes.

In the fussing that Morrison describes, I see Mama's proclivity to amplify the given, her sensual touch or handling – of the doilies and the fragrances of the dresser, her curation of the china in the dining-room cabinet, her sewing of beautiful garments, her polishing of floors and furniture, her use of essential oils of mint and rosemary – that transformed her reality before her eyes, and mine. And if it didn't instantly, miraculously, strip away difficulty, it was also a way of forcing oneself to catch up with the reality of the dream, of 'tricking' one's mind into inhabiting a reality of beauty. Yes, Mama forced herself to dream. I say 'forced herself', but I think there must also have been a pleasure there. Certainly, the tenderness, the beauty, of her surroundings spoke of pleasure. I wonder whether beauty isn't a *story* we tell to ourselves, about ourselves. A story about our bodies' rightness. So that every expression of that story is a refusal of violence. I think Christina Sharpe might agree. She asks: *What is beauty made of?* Her own answer: *Attentiveness whenever possible to a kind of aesthetic that escaped violence whenever possible.*

The deep connection with the land has always been central to this pursuit of beauty, to the evading of violence. From a certain perspective, this relationship is one of constraint – the land is all we have, the land has everything we have; our technologies are fashioned in conjunction with the land. Bush technologies. But isn't it more than this? Through bush technologies, we exercise and express our love for the land, our embeddedness in it; we experience ourselves as part of the green and ochre ecology of our land. Our ecology is *us*. This is how I think of salindine. When I type this into Google, it gives me *celandine*, but that plant has nothing to do with the large shrub with cleft edges that grows on our hillsides. It is one of many plants that are illustrative to me now of the ways in which our bush technology was inseparable from our way of life, of how plants connected the earth and the home.

Mama, like so many others, would use the leaves of the salindine plant to clean and beautify the floors of her dwelling. They'd wipe the board floor clean before rubbing the leaves of the salindine tree all over and letting the floor dry. When it had dried, they'd use the coconut brush to buff it. It would be resplendent. *When it done shine*, Mama used to say, *you suppose to can see you face inna it.* This was an instruction to the girl, my mother, who performed her many chores around the home. It wasn't done right until you could see your reflection in the floor. *But,* my mother adds, as children *it used to be our pleasure, because, after we finished shining the floor, we would put down a piece of cloth on it, on which we would skate. We'd just skate on the floor, like we crazy. That was our fun.* If they fell, the board floor wouldn't hurt them. After the floor was *shined,* entering with shoes was strictly forbidden (children often didn't wear them in those days, anyway). Spread out at the front of the house, there would always be a piece of cloth – an old dress or skirt, a pair of trousers – for wiping your feet, because after you cleaned that floor, you dared not go in and smear it.

The salindine grew on hillsides; the plant likes such areas. Mama would use it immediately after gathering it, and I would luxuriate in the greenness of its cedar-like aroma. It was never used for tea or for drinking, only to clean the floor. Now that people no longer pick it to clean their floors, it's just there. The animals don't eat it. The elders say that anything the goats don't eat is poisonous. In the plant world, everything has its purpose, and our people know. At least, they *have* known. So much of that knowledge is vanishing.

I wonder, who were the first persons to decide to clean their floors this way? I say to my mother. *The first people who discovered that this thing made floors gleam and said to themselves, 'We're going to use it'?* I know such questions will yield no specific answers; still, I ask them as a way of thinking about the intentionality of the practice, and because I fancy they may help me delve deeper in my understanding of bush technology, of our particular inventiveness and our practice of beauty. *It goes way back,* my mother ventures. *I think the*

main reason they used it was because they couldn't afford polish;
or maybe 'polish', as we know it, didn't even exist back then. Yes,
our people were using salindine before floor polish was even
invented, perhaps even before they used beeswax on floors,
rubbing the wax on the coconut brush itself before rubbing
the floor with it. Shining – this compulsion to make surfaces
gleam.

The sheen generated by the salindine would be even
deeper if Mama first dyed the cedar-board floor of her
Coffee Grove home with the dye she made from the bullet
tree, chipping its bark and boiling it.

As Mommy brings the renovations closer to completion, it
feels good to know that I'll have somewhere of my own to
stay whenever I visit this place. It's a dark night tonight.
The cold front sitting over the island forces me to don my
sweater as I go outside. The view of the starry sky moves
me to breathe the word *welcome* to myself – welcome, Jason,
to this vaulted tapestry; welcome back to Coffee Grove and
to dark starry nights like this. The last Coffee Grove dark
night is in the recesses of my memory, yet as I unlock the
grille and walk out into the yard, it becomes so immediate.
Venus is going down from where I look up. I can still see it
through the top of an avocado tree. It was only recently
that I first learned that this brightest of stars is Venus, the
one seen before all others appear, even when the sky is a bit
polluted. *The Shepherd's Star.* I wonder what people who
speak no European language call this star. I wonder what I
ever called it as a child. What name did any child or any
adult have for it back home?

What name does a thing have when it becomes present to
your body, as if something quietly acting on you, shaping

you one night at a time, one instant at a time? What names do the brightest and biggest stars have when you see them on dark nights in the hills, in villages that have no electric light, and you can almost reach up and hold them? They are in you – you have no names for them.

Do you hold less knowledge, because you did not store up the names of things?

But perhaps you did have names for all the things whose names you do not know. Perhaps. But in a language you learned to unlearn. A language that became loose, less fixed in your mind, though not on your tongue, because you were taught that it was inadequate for naming, unscientific, that it couldn't hold the prestige of *Venus*, or of the things fixed in Greek, things that extolled another civilisation.

But now you think you'd like to retrieve the names you had for things in your own language, the one banished from your classrooms at school, the language of the dark nights and the bottle-torch-lit roads, the language of pattoos and stars – lots of stars that you could touch – always present to you because there was so much silence. So much *space to hear*. Where things always had the chance to speak for themselves, in their own language.

The following evening, I walk towards Mama's house with the intention of walking past it, with the desire to be aimless. There's a sort of rambling way of moving through the landscape that always feels generative to me, a sort of affirmation of the connections between body and place; it's the ultimate sign of freedom. I'm still thinking about Mama's aesthetics, her dream attitude, the story she told about herself; about how she cared for me. Yesterday, as I rested in Miss Carmen's shop, Dagu, a Parkinson, one of the young guys she used to share banter with, reminded me how she used to get the goat's milk and scald it to feed me after my mother left me with her at one week old. *That old woman take care of you as if you was her only child* was what he said solemnly, looking me in the eye.

I come upon the house now at the brow of the hill. I can see it clearly in the moonlight. It's empty. Big bay windows installed. Gonna let in a lot of sunlight. I can imagine the future life of the house. But it's just empty and she's no longer there. And the whole of that history, the whole of my childhood, is happening again in this moment. I encounter it again now. The voice of Mama, the sound of Mama.

I encounter, too, the little old woman sitting down on the veranda, patient, looking out, waiting. I remember, Mama, how you used to just sit there on your bench, on the veranda, and look. There was so much silence in your life, and in that time, and you were so comfortable with so much of it. People would pass, wave and call your name, *Sister Morgan! How you do?!*, and you'd reply, *Looking pon you, the better one!* Or Dagu, the Parkinson boy whom you liked so much, he was your little friend, would cry out, *Pretty!* and you'd shout back, *Ugly!*

And when I'd come back to see you, after a long time, after one of my long sojourns far away, first in Kingston, then overseas – France, Martinique, the Bahamas, Canada – something would rise visibly inside you, though you'd never get up off your stool. You'd just sit there, smiling, pretending you didn't know who had come back home, even when you'd already recognised me. Sometimes it did take a while for you to recognise me, as your eyesight grew fainter. But whatever effusiveness there was, was in your smile. Your eyes beaming and probably a little moist. *Eh-eh*, you'd say, your African onomatopoeias coming out to express both surprise and excess of emotion. *Mi think say you woulda neva come . . .* Then you'd say, *You put on likkle weight . . .* Sometimes you'd even say, *What a way you fat!* And then I'd know you were very satisfied with my appearance. You'd say things like that. When I was at university, you'd say, *Then a how you mawga so? It look like you a starve up de. You not getting anything fi eat?* You'd say things like that to temper your emotion: deflection. Yet you couldn't hide from it entirely. *You think a little call me call your name . . . Tommy! Tommy?!* You'd lay in, using my pet name, the only one by which you ever called me. *You think a little pray me pray.* You'd of course use the phrase you used the most: you'd say, *How mi fret!* Fret, you were always fretting for me, your one Tommy, the boy child you wanted in your own youth but never had – I'd become him. And you'd remind me, *How a me raise you.* As if you were afraid I'd forget. *From you one week old, me have you up and down, on mi back. I have you when mi going to Post Office, day in day out, come rain or shine.*

The last time I saw you was the September of 2011, when I migrated to England to take up my scholarship. Your dementia was already becoming obvious. In the year that followed, my first year at Oxford, it became even more pronounced. I imagine you in the care home where Mommy placed you, having no alternative options. I imagine you sitting on the bed; all you're doing now with the time is sitting, lying down and looking. The place where you were was not somewhere one could reach. Yet you waited, hoping, from that distant place, that I would find you, as you reached out to me. But I did not come, did I? I was in Paris, busy reinventing myself.

★

Are you proud of the transformation, Mama?

In this yard on the brow of the hill, I meet you again, as if you were waiting all over again, as if you have never stopped. How often will I come to encounter your ghost in this manner and how long will it be before this pang gets duller?

But mixed up within that pang are the pride, the joy, the knowledge that this house will soon be inhabited again. It will take on a different life. Aren't you happy that Mommy is building up the house? Are you sad or proud that it's being transformed so much to become a different house? Can this house be the same house?

Now, memory becomes all of past time in one instant. In my memory, there are many, many years that become an ocean, and I do not know how to locate myself within it. The ocean has no geography, only a compelling, an exclamation; an overwhelming, almost tangible, sense of presence – yours.

Hadn't realised how much I had missed having my hands in dirt, how much I had missed the touch of things that flake, drip, run, soil, stain. Welcome back, messy things. I had forgotten how much I luxuriate in the touch of you. How much I luxuriate in that crumby, crusty breadnut bark.

In my study in Leeds, I open a cloth bag containing bissy, Jamaican dandelion and ramoon. I want to make a tea from the ramoon. As I break off a piece of the bark, the crust flakes and releases brown dust onto my green Ikea sofa, onto my books, onto a letter from the Virginia Museum of Fine Art. The dust is out of place in this environment. I would rather it were not there. I've been thinking about the need to have surfaces clean and tidy for when my wife returns with the kids.

But for now, I leave the dust on the sofa, on the letter, on the books. For the lost pleasure of the dirt.

On the Veranda of the Great House

As our guide, Jenny, leads us on the tour, I cannot help thinking about scale, vantage points and verandas. This visit to Greenwood Great House in St James marks my last significant outing before returning to Leeds and reuniting with my family.

I want to remember just how much land was owned by the Barretts, the slave-owning family that built this great house. Jenny informs us that their estates stretched from Little River in St James, somewhere near where we currently are, all the way to Falmouth in Trelawny: 84,000 acres of land. 'Their land'. Staggering – the very idea that this English family 'owned' the land, that it could be called 'theirs'. Jenny tells us about the number of slaves they owned – more than two thousand – and how they were known to be 'humane masters'; they were known to treat their slaves well, she says. 'The Barretts were the rare kinds of masters who taught their slaves to read.'

In this room, the study, I become struck by the portrait of the man who built the house, Mr Richard Barrett, cousin to Edward Barrett. At the time Greenwood Great House was built, the family also owned a house in London, the site of which, located near present-day Selfridges, is still known as Barrett Street. The Barretts were among the very first English settlers of this island – the patriarch, Hersey

Barrett, was an officer in the expedition commanded by Penn and Venables that captured Jamaica from the Spanish in 1655. The website of Greenwood Great House tells me that Hersey was 'granted lands in Jamaica' for his role in the expedition.

As I look at the portrait of Richard, its out-of-placeness seems both a kind of magic and a sort of mystery. I note how the demeanour and attire of this man contrast with the reality of the slave labour that marked and dominated this land. The parallel reality of gentility, high society, food, leisure, music, transplanted English culture and faux-aristocratic manners, this grotesque sense of play happening among the whites who had become a new class in a so-called new world – all this world existed in parallel to the world of their slaves. This reality strikes me with strange and startling physicality, as if the spirit of this absurd time has manifested itself suddenly in my body, or in the space, extending its tightness all around me. I feel the cruel, strange absurdity, an absurdity so uncanny as to almost produce laughter – a gift of tragedy stored up by one age and offered to another, as if that earlier age were incapable of viewing itself, as if the near artistry of its own evil were lost on itself. I'm feeling it now in the images on the wall, in particular in this portrait of Mr Richard Barrett, which seems like something I might have looked at in the National Portrait Gallery in London, where it would have seemed at home, in its own context. Or in one of the many stately homes of the English countryside, though the irony of this is that all the British stately homes I've visited seem to lead back to the plantations of the Americas – coffee, sugar, cotton, wood, indigo . . . the West Indies, the British North American colonies, Guyana.

★

I've never thought much about the strangeness of the images within the 'plantation museums' we have inherited, which were, of course, anything but museums for my ancestors and their masters who inhabited them, or about the strangeness of the images of the plantation.

These buildings are tourist attractions; there is an abstraction to the images, an abstraction of the grotesque absurdity that they embody. To recognise this absurdity might be to alienate the tourists, these white working-class consumers of sand, sea and *yeah mon*; it might make them uncomfortable. Many of the great houses are in the private hands of wealthy, upper-class, light-skinned Jamaicans, some of them descendants of the same people who owned the land two hundred years ago. These houses form part of a sizeable wealth-generating economy, as the 'attractions' can also be rented for weddings and other social gatherings that frequently make the 'society' pages of the local newspapers. Tourism, paradise, socialites.

I'm struck by the images thrown up by the great house: images of who we are as a people, and of who can naturally be seen in these spaces, on their extravagantly long and spacious verandas, on their manicured lawns. Images of vantage points and viewing privileges.

Jenny, the tour guide, is a dark-skinned, bespectacled woman of average height, with hair in neat cornrows. She's not the usual tour guide. Her English, riding on her musical Jamaican accent, is grammatically precise, lively and effortless. I imagine her to be a retired teacher who, throughout her entire life, has cultivated a curiosity about the world and her own space in it, in this patch on earth called Jamaica. She recounts details about the great house and the lives of those who've inhabited it since its construction. She evokes

Elizabeth Barrett Browning, the English poet, heiress and cousin to Richard. Though Elizabeth never ventured to Jamaica, Jenny tells us, it was the income of £4,000 brought in by her father Edward's plantations in 1807 that enabled him to purchase the 500-acre Hereford estate on which his daughter would grow up. We also learn from Jenny that the two main Barrett-owned estates in this parish of Trelawny, named somewhat hilariously (despite the tragic subject matter) Oxford and Cambridge, were bequeathed to Elizabeth in Edward's 1798 will.

Jenny speaks about numbers of slaves, their occupations, the work they did in this house, the spaces in which they worked. She speaks about regalia and paraphernalia, about grand objects, about the mahogany desks of the study, about a piano crafted by John Broadwood, an eighteenth-century piano maker who famously gifted one of his instruments to Beethoven in 1813, and about an oak chair bearing ornately carved reliefs. Shipped from Belgium, a chair like this would have been used to augment the weight of a slave ship's 'cargo', reducing the amount of ballast needed. (At the time, ballast usually consisted of rocks and the hewn stones used for making these very great houses.) She names the individuals in the portraits, speaks of the places and lands they owned, the marriage alliances they formed, and describes the histories of land ownership of this small island, linking it to the faces, ghosts in a certain way, of this great house. Mapping the who's who of the Jamaican plantocracy from the rooms of this great house, from the ground we stand on.

It is significant that a knowledgeable woman is doing this tour, a woman not just doing this for a job, it seems, but out of a real passion and commitment to the memory that attends this place. It is significant that a descendant of slaves is speaking to other descendants of slaves. We are not tourists. And so our gasps and sighs speak of a shared history, of a coming together around something that unites us; we have a stake in this so-called great house, and during this tour we form a kind of kinship with each other.

When the formal tour is over, I ask her permission to go back up onto the veranda. It's a long shot, I think, but somehow I feel pressed to do this; the least I can do is ask. I explain my motive – I want to photograph myself in that space. I'm drawn to these long, spacious verandas with their Georgian fretwork; I'm fascinated by their extravagance, and the fact that, in the great houses I've seen, these verandas tower over the hillsides below and often have a grand view of the sea. I'm fascinated by the narrative of space that's being told by these verandas and want to feel myself stand within them in an owner's stance. I want to experience what it might feel like to own this space, to stand looking out with the knowledge that this place is my rightful place, that nothing assails my right of ownership of this vantage point; that nothing could. Might it be possible for me to know how that feels? Somehow, on this day, I am impelled to try to enact this performance. *Could I become a white planter for a moment, feel his embodiment in my flesh?*

Perched high on the hill, the veranda commands a view of the landscape below. As I stand here, I can't help but wonder: What would the house's inhabitants have seen in 1800, when its construction was complete? A sugar-cane plantation? Mills, presses, ploughs, beasts of burden? I do not know what the exact layout of the land below the house would have been. The great house was used primarily for entertainment, though I do know that Cinnamon Hill, with its sugar plantation built by Samuel Barrett Jr, is only twelve kilometres away. Like Greenwood, like so many other great houses on this island, Cinnamon Hill overlooks the sea. Would the colonising European viewer have looked out on sugar works, woodlands, a network of roads linking properties, leading to the sea? How many African bodies would have been there? The privilege of viewing was also the privilege of space, of control over the land and over that *other* territory – the enslaved African body.

I gaze out through the wide, flung-open windows before stepping onto the sprawling veranda of the time portal that is this manor. What I see below me is a chaotic jumble of houses that seems to have sprung from a manic imagination. A visual depiction of our history, of its dramatic form. This contemporary landscape, suggesting an unsettled calamity, is akin to a palimpsest – a manuscript with layers of writing that have been partially erased and overwritten. Isolating its myriad layers is a daunting task. Yet, amidst this complexity, one cannot escape the palpable sensation of multiple temporal strata converging into a singular block of time, with the construction of this great house being just one facet of its intricate mass. Down on the hill, the descendants of slaves now – clearly – have the right to own property and build houses of their own.

To look down on these dwellings below is to view what, for the Barretts, would have been the lesser people. In seeking to enter and inhabit that perspective, I can't help but consider how it must have felt to be scrutinised by the white planter surveying his domain from the veranda high above. I feel resentment. I feel anger. For so much has been stolen from us. And I can't undo that. Spatially, this is a poignant materialisation of what slavery has produced.

The boundaries between owners and dispossessed have

blurred over time. The descendants of slaves are constantly trying to move further and further up the hill. That's our determination. The dream of the big house is the fantasy of having that same expansive vista as the great house, such an all-embracing visual clasp of territory, or simply the ambiguous claim of poor Black people to luxury and to what's been existentially denied them for centuries – land. The viewer standing on this veranda in 1800 could not have imagined a sight like this.

In their chaos, in the desperate ambition that they embody, the constructions below seem to emerge from each other, like infinitely proliferating beings. There is no end to how big they will be, as people compete to outdo each other with three- and four-storey houses, broad villas with swimming pools, palatial fortresses. All these lie among and alongside tawdry mansions, exaggerated structures owned by people whose ambitions far outstrip their means. One is struck by the imperatives of splendour, the pretensions to grandeur that inhabit these builders. The grandeur of power, property and visibility is the presence of the great house that haunts the mind like a spectre.

Yet, two hundred years later, the great house itself still enjoys the commanding view and privileged position by virtue of being built by white colonists who decided that all the privileges of the land should be theirs. It's exhausting to dwell within this historical framework, one that continues to shape our lives and perceptions. And yet the prospect of breaking free from its confines remains elusive.

Here, I'm far from Coffee Grove. Yet I find myself drawn to reflect on the place of my birth. Despite the geographical disparity, parallels emerge between this coastal enclave and the hillsides of Coffee Grove, both reflecting the evolving relationship between land and the Black majority. Beneath these surface resemblances lies a stark divergence – the allure of the coast, coveted for its proximity to the sea. Here a particular narrative unfolds, shaped by distinct aspirations and yearnings for ownership of 'prime real estate'.

I'm reminded of a university friend who has erected a beautiful and spacious residence on this very hillside. People's progress and upward mobility. This mass of concrete, which is also an environmental tragedy, is the excrescence of our history of dispossession. But for the people looking out at the sea from their big houses, it may be difficult to see anything but a certain kind of order, a sense of their body now being in the right place. The expansive view from the hill now also belongs to them. It's all deeply ambivalent, of course.

Amidst this reflection, a sobering truth emerges – the plantation and the peasant plot symbolise two separate modes of cultivation, inexorably intertwined with the brutal legacy of slavery. For the plantation, the enslavement of Africans is at the root of the capitalist model of production that would power the Industrial Revolution. Some would say that model of production is still with us today, despite evident permutations. The plot undoubtedly hinges on physical labour, yet it depends equally on creativity. It's not merely about the bare body, bare life, as on the plantation. Here, the body isn't reduced to brute force and toil, perceived as mere chattel. To work the land and live alongside it often involves a profound creative spirit, especially when this land is not deemed 'prime real estate' – when it's less useful for exploitative purposes and therefore more defended against capitalism. In other words, to dwell alongside the land in a positive, life-affirming way is a creative act, and this is what I've tried to show through the people I've portraited, the narratives I've told.

The aesthetics of the great house prevent us from seeing those forms of creativity. By being what seems normal, they hide their own violence, enforcing social mores, a norm – creating the idea of what is good, cultured, beautiful. By being beautiful, the great house hides the violence that exists in the margins of its beauty. I guess it took coming to stand here to be able to put this into words. I'm training myself to stop viewing Coffee Grove through the lens of the great house – through the lens of what its vantage point stands for. This is what this search for plants and dreams has been about, after all. From the perspective of the great house, one learns to adopt a lens tinted with disregard – perhaps even contempt. You learn to look down on those you consider lowly; you have disdain for those who have their hands in the soil. The search for the plants, via Mama, has taught me to look and see from a different perspective, retraining not merely my eyes but my mind. Now, for me, the aesthetics of the grung no longer exist in the shadow of the great house but in their own right. They exist *in spite of* the great house.

In my journey, I've shown both the ardour and the arduousness of the grung. I've shown the beauty and the slog of the walk. The grung is non-romantic. Sitting with the soil, I've done my utmost to avoid the 'happy nature' version of what it means to plant and grow things, but, really, it wasn't difficult at all. I've wanted to show how arduousness need not be antithetical to the pleasure of the land.

The pleasure of the land is visceral – for Congolin, Mommy, Miss Ivey, as it was for Mama. Part of that pleasure is simply the joy of being with it, despite the discomfort that sometimes comes with this. It's the ease with which they inhabit the land, are naturally part of it and relate to it. In the West, this has become a luxury. People who are supposedly prosperous, whose incomes are twenty times Congolin's, are still divorced from the wealth that is land. This ease of inhabiting land has made me far more aware of the diminishing of the dreaming pleasure of land in the West.

As I close this phase of the journey, I'm reminded of the way Congolin moves around on his plot, how he talks about and looks at it – with pride. As I observed him, I mused to myself that it was probably the way aristocrats talked about their land, with pride and satisfaction, while moving around on it. The way a very tiny handful of people still do. Yet, with Congolin, there was something that went beyond pride and satisfaction. It was like desire, a connection coming from the knowledge that not only does the land belong to you, but you belong to it as well – a sense of reciprocity.

It's this sense of reciprocity that's been stripped from people in England – and, by extension, the West. The widening of the proletariat, rapid urbanisation and the violence of enclosures have all contributed to this loss. People have been deprived of the ability to envision a relationship with the land built around mutual care and stewardship. Significantly, what people have been deprived of is the ability to *imagine* being with the land, living in harmony with it, as many of their distant ancestors once did. And, as I've already mentioned, land kinship is dream space. There's a space for dreaming that's so tied to having the earth, to *being* earthed.

If Coffee Grove is important, it's also because it helps us to understand how that possibility of being earthed has been lost. By looking at the story of land in my small district, I've seen, poignantly, how much the disenfranchisement of people from land in Britain is contingent on the disenfranchisement of a whole set of people from the global majority. Just the history of coffee in the former slave plantation that is Coffee Grove is enough to show that. Henry Thomas De la Beche simply coming to map the geology of my island in order to stem the economic fallout from revolts and slaves running away into the island's hilly interior is enough to illustrate it. If we only consider Greenwood Great House, then widen the lens to look at land wealth in Britain and how much of it has been generated by the plantations, through slavery and the slave trade, we can understand the connections with crystal clarity.

So, if I've tried to *write grung* in a non-romanticised way, not 'the simple beauty of the simple people working the earth' kind of thing, it's to show us – myself and you, my reader – how much the place, people and history that are Coffee Grove can transform the way we see and imagine. The intimacy I feel with the land of that place is what's helping me to imagine my body bigger than a racialised body, but also to imagine my body empowered by the connections with the soil that I can actively form.

It may not be possible at all to live beyond History, but the ability to *see* myself beyond it is what I feel the plants offer me. In my search, I started to perceive the plants as individuals in their own right. And from that moment, it became important for me to try to portray them as fully drawn characters, much like the individuals I encountered along my journey. And now, after reconnecting with my roots and embracing the wisdom of my people regarding plants, I'm ready to explore even more ways of engaging with them.

Understanding just how much constellates around them has shifted my systemic understanding of the world we live in.

I bring back dozens of them with me from Jamaica, gifts from Congolin as parting tokens, vade mecums, if you will. These plants are more than mementos; they foster our connection and are intended for my health and well-being, to help me remain grounded in the soil. I carefully pack the dried herbs in my suitcases, considering them some of my most precious possessions. When I make teas with them, the aromas bring back memories of Coffee Grove's soil. I'd say *in my mind*, but it's also as if I'm physically there. Amidst the hustle and bustle of my life in Leeds, the smell of the herbs boiling on the stove in the mornings instils in me a sense of calm and reassurance about my place, my powerful place, in the universe.

Yesterday, I took a bath with patchouli, vervain and wild basil, and I was overwhelmed by a feeling that's hard to put into words. The plants stay with me, even in my dreams. They're there when I awake, a feeling in my chest. Their presence is a powerful, bubbling impulse in my body, making me feel whole and capable of anything. I'm entire, I'm powerful. My destiny is larger than I can even imagine. Nothing could ever make me doubt my worth, my purpose, my rightness in this place where I currently live, work and dream. I feel an immense power radiating from within, so strong it makes me want to do cartwheels. Instead, I channel this energy into every cell of my being, calming it to a hum, knowing it serves me, my family, my friends and my community. I'm increasingly exploring the curative and restorative power of herbs, finding transformative experiences in the sanctuaries I create in my home.

So it's not just about ingesting teas, but also about how my body connects with the plants in a new, dynamic cosmovision – through baths, through care for the body, through the atmospheres I create in my home with their fragrances; through the time taken to deepen my connections with ancestry and with the earth. I honour my body through them, practising reciprocity by welcoming them into every facet of my life.

By incorporating them into my personal space, I acknowledge their power and our interdependence with the living world. Yearning for a connection that transcends the physical, I invite them to immerse me in a new vision in which they're active, aware and engaged. I never imagined that I'd desire such closeness with the plants, that I'd yearn for them to connect with me through the pores of my body.

Contemplating the profound impact of plant immersion, I set off on a new phase of my journey, discovering new ones and learning how communities in Africa and its diaspora live with and from them. That's what Mama, and so many of the other characters on this journey, have offered me. The gateway to a new form of living, at this stage of life, after so many years of wandering, of roving away from my small place.

Epilogue

The first tiny bloom had opened. It had called her to come and gaze on a mystery. From barren blown stems to glistening leaf-buds; from the leaf-buds to snowy virginity of bloom. It stirred her tremendously. How? Why? It was like a flute song forgotten in another existence and remembered again. What? How? Why? This singing she heard that had nothing to do with her ears.

—Zora Neale Hurston

I am walking in Roundhay Park. My previous self, the self I was when I moved to live on the edges of this park in January 2019, was taken with things I don't notice any more: the green moss that covers a stone, the sight of a bare tree in the half-light of dusk. That self took photos of such things. I can picture what I must have looked like when I first moved to the park and took up walking, what my interior world must have been like – the picture, or the musical composition, of seeing a new world of lively things. A *second life of seeing*.

Today's the fourth of January of yet another year living in this locale. I'm watching men in high-vis jackets dismantle the holiday winter wonderland, with all of its lights in the lake and woods. I don't come here often any more; in fact, I hardly come at all. That said, I've been trying to get into the woods for the past week and a half and have not been able to, because of the iron barricades forming a contour around them. You have to pay, and quite a lot, too, to enter the winter wonderland set up in this public park.

I have started finding it impossible to retrieve those early joys, the exhilaration of encountering and knowing this park and its woodlands. I marvel now at how magical I found those early days, when I moved to Roundhay in January 2019. It's the magic of that first wonder – which feels like a first experience of the world – that the character Janie experiences in Zora Neale Hurston's *Their Eyes Were Watching God*: 'The rose of the world was breathing out smell. It followed her through all her waking moments and caressed her in her sleep.' And because of this sentiment, and because of the entire journey I've been on – my *second childhood of seeing* – I can't help but think about my own daughter, who's now six, who was a toddler when we did all that walking in Roundhay Park as a way of remaining healthy and sane during the pandemic, as a way of doing *something*. The park was all that we had as a living space, 'nature', a place to escape the confinement of those oppressive days. It was in those days that Leyla, this first child of mine, learned walking. Because we're in a culture where people 'go walking', unlike in her father's district of Coffee Grove, a place unknown to her. And because she's a child of parents who can afford to go walking, who have enough time on their hands. Her father has changed class. How much of this will she understand? But watching her see the world from her height, with wonder in her eyes, watching her discover the touch of bark, of earth, of grass, of wild plants, led me to yearn again for my own childhood wonder, to try to imagine, relive, what it might have been. The experience of watching her produced, too, this feeling of living a childhood again. I looked at Leyla:

mindsliding
in the sticky
film of the bud
rubbing her thoughts
between
fingers

and knowing the
purple lips of the
involucres in her mouth

Watching Leyla makes me think about what status 'nature' had for us as children in Coffee Grove. The first time I heard the word was in secondary school – science class? Did I read it in a biology textbook? We have no way of thinking of ourselves outside of our relationship with the plants, with the earth and the things that we grow. We have no term for a life that exists in isolation from the 'bush', 'bush' being simply, for us, the uncleared forest. 'Nature' denotes a separation, a way of naming something that exists apart from you. A symptom of this embeddedness was that our lives were often characterised by labour, albeit not the kind of labour that was devoid of joy – but let's face it, farming is hard work; living from the soil entails toil. Our parents knew no such thing as 'leisure'; the concept didn't exist.

★

I recall that it was Leyla who made me realise what a pine cone was, and that there was, for me, something of the childhood wonder in that moment. It happened on one of our daily walks during the pandemic. It suddenly dawned on me:

A pine cone . . .
is what I had on the night table in my bedroom in Porus.
For the first time I realise.
Donovan had received it –
I shared a bedroom with Donovan, my mother's ward –
Who sent it, I do not know . . .
Some relative? Somebody come home from foreign?
Sent by his mother in a barrel?
Revealed to me here by my child doing nothing
but running
up and down the dark lane, throwing pine cones and
peering over the hillside at people passing.
Now she's shouting *daddy daddy my pine cone,*
my pine cone has rolled down to the bottom.
She's not even three, my daughter, saying *my pine cone.*

And now we're going down the ravine in search of her lost
    pine cone.
Yes, a child just playing with the woods
has revealed to me the mystery of that wooden flower
or that flower-like piece of wood
that lay on the night table in the bedroom
I shared with Donovan.

As for me, I was silent at the time, so mute
that I was unable to ask a question about this flower.

That ornament, Donovan's,
was a curious thing;
it didn't belong to our landscape,

and only today – after all, I'm still learning all this flora and
fauna and thinking how I must connect with this nature
and these trees and plants and birds – only now does my
daughter, she for whom playing with pine cones is the
most natural thing in the world, only now does she make
me see

the thing that that thing was.

What strikes me as exotic is entirely natural to Leyla.
While I find the rediscovery of childhood sensations revo-
lutionary, I'm reminded that childhood also entails taking
things for granted. Leyla effortlessly embodies this notion,
her appreciation of the pine cone both casual and profound. Observing her innate connection with the pine cone
prompts reflections on transplantation. For Leyla, this
closeness to the landscape here is intrinsic; it requires no
conscious effort to root herself in this soil, unlike my own
experience. Her distinct relationship with the land and
soil stems from factors like migration, her father's in part,
and socio-economic class. Yet I find solace in knowing that
certain lessons, less readily absorbed here, can be imparted
by me. It's comforting to realise that we can learn from
each other.

I've just walked past a section of the wood that I hadn't
visited in years, perhaps not since the days of the pandemic.
I see an overturned tree. A slope. Lots of red leaves. And

then the coolness of a spreading tree, the protectiveness of the long limbs. It was there that Leyla and I stopped on a series of days during the first lockdown. And what I remember most is Leyla playing, oblivious of the aggressions that her dad contends with daily. I remember her pram; I'm surprised that I managed to come all the way here with it. The determination it took to push that pram over all the roots of all the hills, in between tight spaces, over rocky ground, to get all the way here. Or perhaps it was a kind of obliviousness, a kind of ignorance of the reasons why one would *not do* such a thing. I'm so surprised at how natural we were, how comfortable we were here. Leyla, at two years old, walked astonishingly long distances. Was it the restrictions of the pandemic that taught her how to walk for so many miles?

I've passed the spot where she and I used to rest. But now I stand up on a tree, reflecting back on that spot where I see Leyla in the negative of this memory's film reel. What strikes me most is the fullness of her contentment, her indulgence in the childhood joy of being in this space. I see Leyla with her Afro, her slightly buck teeth, her rubicund face, the glittering pools of her smile. I hear her parakeet laugh, the sound of her feet pattering on the ground of the slope. She plays under the tree, with leaves, touching bark, rubbing her hands over things.

I see both of us playing hide-and-seek in this pandemic wood. I also see all the people who pass. Family after family, they feel this familiar feeling of stuckness, of having nothing else to do but come out. They discover spaces of the backwoods into which they would not ordinarily have come. They're passing the time. They pass us. Only a look or a swift dart of the eyes acknowledges that we're here. English awkwardness. Leyla, oblivious. The fullness of her play becomes even fuller in that moment. Stark relief, childhood play. In the negative of this film, I am thrilled for the thriving of my daughter in the green space.

It's my first time round here in well over two years. I'm standing on an overturned tree. I'm sitting now, so as to be less threatening to the people passing by. I'm sitting down on the tree to love the tree, but also to more easily occupy my space. The tree seems so undead. All that I said above, I said while standing on the trunk. I went up on the trunk, thinking. This was my way out of history.

On this winter weekday morning, I see well-formed trails and beaten footpaths, but no people. Slipping back to that winter I first set foot in this place, I see the floor of dry leaves that glinted like so many coins. Today I'm going the full distance of a trail I used to take during the pandemic, often running, sometimes walking with Leyla or by myself.

It's so strange, when you think about it, for me to be here, walking. For me to be out of Coffee Grove and here in Leeds, walking, not with my goats but just walking. Living in a house in Leeds is already far away; walking in these woods is like being on another planet. And yet . . . My life is now wedded to this place. Both my children were born in this country. I'm opening myself up now to the possibility of tenderness in this soil of transplantation. To the idea that I might somehow walk here the way I learned to walk as a child. Somehow. Through some means. It might not be here in the park, but it might be somewhere out there with new friends.

It's approaching dusk. I'm standing on a bend in a narrow walking path, typing notes on my phone, a possible segment for a book. A young man with a walking pole approaches, he's upon me before I even hear him. The dried leaves crackle under his footsteps. He looks down. He looks into the shrubbery of holly; he asks all the holly to welcome his body. What would have happened if we'd said hello to each other? I resume walking, then stop again to type, and after quite a while I hear the sound of wood on rock and turn around. An old Black man is approaching behind me. I continue typing. I am exhilarated. He does not look at me, he does not say hello. He sends his walking stick, and his eyes, into the ground. But I will not miss the opportunity to speak to him, and to myself. I say, *Sir, I'm glad to see you here; it means everything to me.* He cracks a very reluctant, sheepish smile, nods and keeps on walking. I recall now one of the questions I posed to myself earlier: *whether beauty isn't a* story *we tell to ourselves, about ourselves.* And indeed, the story I'm telling to myself, about myself, now, is this: *I'm glad to see you here.*

I continue my walk, arriving at a slope surrounded by densely packed trees. I'm meditating on the rhododendrons running like snakes, and a woman overtakes me with her canine in hand, looks back and smiles *good morning,* as if to say it's pleasant to see that you, too, are here, as if to say well done, you've done what's needed. Stay here. It's good for you. And I think, this is what it is to rest. This is what Mama was seeking; what my mother, too, was seeking. Rest. The ability to be here, to walk through the woods, on the leaves. The ability not to think of space, but to inhabit it – unhindered, unbarred. Through the numerous trunks of trees, under the bellies of rhododendrons. Time is not upon us – the woman's *good morning* is a shared affirmation of rest. I'm in it. And I had never imagined what it might be.

A Note on Sources

Throughout the writing of this book, I consulted a range of sources. I have done my utmost to acknowledge each one within the book itself. However, some of the more salient ones deserve to be highlighted here.

I'm particularly thankful for the work of Christina Sharpe, especially her book *Ordinary Notes*. I'm also grateful for Saidiya Hartman's *Wayward Lives, Beautiful Experiments* and her magnificent essay 'Venus in Two Acts'. These works were instrumental in helping me find the right way to tell the story of Mama. Alice Walker's *In Search of Our Mothers' Gardens* and the poetry of Lorna Goodison in general were also significant in this regard. Teju Cole's writing in *Human Archipelago* and *Blind Spot* suggested ways of writing the visual aspects of Coffee Grove's landscapes, between the instinct of familiarity and the impulse of one seeing them, as it were, for the first time.

There were so many books that dealt with history, land, geology, the environment, the peasantry, food growing and related concerns. Perhaps the most significant for me were those of Dr Erna Brodber. Her sociological studies of Black peasant Jamaicans (including *Woodside, Pear Tree Grove P.O.*), as well as her novels, which often double as sociological material, were crucial. Hours spent speaking with Dr Brodber not only enriched this book but also shaped the questions I asked about the land in Jamaica and my ways of approaching the archives.

The work of E. P. Thompson was significant, as was Nick Hayes' *The Book of Trespass*, which helped me draw connections between the land question in modern Britain and Jamaica's colonial history. Corinne Fowler's work, particularly *Green Unpleasant Land* and her more recent *Our Island Stories*, deepened my understanding of these connections, in parallel with my own archival research in Jamaica.

Other instrumental books include Dénètem Touam Bona's *Fugitive, Where Are You Running?* and Tricia Hersey's *Rest is Resistance*. They both helped me articulate significant issues.

The novels of Annie Ernaux nourished my thinking. The work of Édouard Louis continues to exert a great influence on me; it was the case in this book. The very idea of 'the possibility of tenderness' came to me while reading Louis' *Combats et métamorphoses d'une femme*. It was immediately clear to me that this was my title and I haven't second-guessed it since.

The work of historian Douglas Hall was one of the important sources in my research around the history of land ownership and of the emergence of the peasantry in Jamaica. That said, the archives with which I spent much time (the Jamaica Archives at Twickenham Park, the Island Record Office, the National Library of Jamaica, the British Library and the database of the Centre for the Study of the Legacies of British Slavery at UCL) yielded tremendous insights into these issues.

Concerning the plants themselves, most of the lore has come from the storytellers and plant lovers I've encountered on my journey. Nevertheless, Ivelyn Harris's *Healing Herbs of Jamaica* was a very useful handbook. Regarding the plants in England, Nicholas Culpeper's *Complete Herbal* provided much valuable insight. I also learned important things from

Plant Medicine: A Collection of the Teachings of Herbalists Christopher Hedley and Non Shaw, edited by Guy Waddell. These complemented the lessons I have learned along the way from my British plant-loving friends.

Acknowledgements

I would like to express my heartfelt thanks to the many friends, colleagues and institutions that have supported this work. First and foremost, I want to thank my partner, Lucile, without whose unwavering support and belief in me this work would not have been possible. Thank you for your constant encouragement and motivation throughout this journey, and for being one of my first readers.

I am deeply grateful to Lemara Lindsay-Prince, my editor and now friend. Your belief in this project from the start, your enthusiasm, and your efforts in shaping this book have been irreplaceable and I'm forever grateful. Thank you for your support and for boosting my confidence.

Much gratitude, as well, to my second editor, Shan Vahidi, whose insights and guidance during the final stages elevated this book to new heights beyond my initial vision.

Many thanks, too, to Helen Conford for your enthusiasm and thoughtful advice, despite your many responsibilities. I truly appreciate the time and space you made for this book.

To Vanessa Phan, Katya Browne and Laurie Ip Fung Chun, and the entire Penguin Random House team, a million thanks for your dedication in putting the book together. Working with each of you has been a special experience, and I am grateful for your support.

I'm blessed to have Harriet Moore, an amazing reader, as my agent. Thanks for the thoughtful attention you pay to my work and for all your efforts in helping me get the best of me out to my readers.

The book has had several early readers and I can't express my gratitude enough to them. On that note, special thanks go to my friend Jacob Ross, who took the time to read a very early version of the manuscript. I am also grateful to Honor Ford Smith for her encouragement and valuable insights at an early phase. To David Scott, I so appreciate you for reading a version of this, as well, and for organising an entire event around it at the Institute for Ideas and the Imagination in Paris. Finally, all my gratitude to Nathaniel Stein, curator at the Cincinnati Art Museum for commissioning a piece that eventually formed the basis of chapter 11.

I would like to acknowledge the British Academy for their Global Convening Grant, 'The Times of a Just Transition', which provided funding for some of the fieldwork and archival research that have been essential to the book.

A heartfelt thank you to my family – to my mother, who accompanied me on many of the walks in Coffee Grove and Mount Pleasant; to my cousins Annalee and Dettylin for providing some of the photographs that have ended up in the book; and to Cousin Jackie for her encouragement.

I extend my deepest appreciation to the plant teachers in Jamaica who shared their invaluable knowledge with me. This book is also dedicated to you: to Congolin, to Miss Ivy, and to all the others.

Shout-out to all the grung people of Coffee Grove who shared love, knowledge and memories with me, pouring their energies into this work: Norrel, May-May and all the others. Besides this, a homage to all the people I bucked up along the road there. To Miss Rita, to Hopeton and to Phil, countless thanks, and much gratitude to Jacqueline Bishop for granting me permission to reproduce a piece from *History at the Dinner Table*.

To my friend, the writer Gerty Dambury, a blissful plate of Colombo with a glass of exquisite rum. Gratitude to you for making space for this work and for enabling my residency at the Centre Culturel AKAZ in Le Gouray, Brittany, where I wrote a significant section of this book.

Thanks to Olive Senior, Lorna Goodison and Erna Brodber, luminaries whose work paved a pathway for my own.

Lastly, thank you to the staff at the National Library of Jamaica; to the wonderful personnel at the Jamaica Archives, particularly Mrs Williams-Pryce; and to Mr Reynolds at the Island Record Office, for your support and assistance.